CURANDERO

A CUENTO

D1611620

CURAN

JOSÉ ORTIZ Y PINO III

DERO

A CUENTO

Sunstone Press
Santa Fe, New Mexico

ACKNOWLEDGEMENTS

To my sister, Maria O. Catanach, in deep appreciation
for allowing me to include her artistry — the retablo sketches.
Her unusual and sensitive style has enhanced this book.

My thanks to Marion Steele for the initial editing of the
manuscript — and also for his great patience.

FIRST EDITION / Printed in the United States of America

Library of Congress Cataloging in Publication Data:

Ortiz y Pino III, José, 1932-
    Curandero: a cuento.

    I. Title.
PS3565.R774C8   1983   813'.54   82-19507
ISBN: 0-86534-020-X

Published in 1983 by SUNSTONE PRESS / Post Office Box 2321 / Santa Fe, New Mexico 87501

DEDICATION

To us who dare dream,
fantasize and cherish our memories —
no one can take them from us, for we have found
the Golden Cities of Cibola.

PROLOGUE

This is a cuento about a people and a time of long ago, a story of the Spanish people whose ancestors settled in Northern New Mexico.

Cuentos are stories which are told over and over again which enchanted audiences and provided entertainment to listeners of all ages. They can be long or short, based on real experiences or made up by the storytellers. Cuentos have been handed down from generation to generation and have become a classic part of New Mexico history.

1880: the year when this story begins was a comparatively tranquil time; life was unhurried but far from easy for these ranchers and their families. Their deep religious beliefs, customs and traditions bound them together. Great changes in their way of life were not to come about until much later.

In this cuento, which is also a love story, is woven the theme of the curandero and the study of medicinal uses and plants, so important in the lives of the people.

As a small child, when I accompanied my father and grandfather on their visits to the many settlements located on their ranch empire, I was fascinated by the cuentos the older men and women related to the younger people. Almost always a short cuento was told about Juanito, the "supreme" curandero: he had a great variety of adventures which provided the young a kind of Saturday-night-at-the-movies serial. Each adventure of Juanito was different and covered a multitude of subjects. One of these stories haunted me. I promised myself someday I would write it so that it would not be lost.

I do not remember if there was a title for this story when I heard it, but I have entitled it *Curandero*.

José Ortiz y Pino III

A   C   U   E   N   T   O

It was that hour before the sun comes to light the adobe walls of the sprawling Ortiz hacienda in the tiny village of San Lucas where Antonio was still asleep. Slowly, the giving way of darkness began and Antonio's world stirred and started to breathe and come to life. First, the chatter of magpies nested in the giant, gnarled cottonwood trees shading the courtyard south of the hacienda and Antonio opened his eyes. Then the distant lowing of the cows and Antonio propped himself on the down-filled pillow—his hands clasped behind his head as he looked out the window.

In the distance, he could see the pale grey sky brighten to a light turquoise. His window faced south so he couldn't see the sunrise; his view was of the budding pear trees in Comadre Juanita's yard across the road. Roosters crowed, serenading the advent of day. Dona Josefa's cow lowed, urging someone to relieve her swollen udder. Flocks of goats and sheep bleated, hungry and ready to start their day of foraging. A dog barked: Lobo, his father's sheep dog.

But Antonio's thoughts were far from these familiar sights and sounds that early day in late May. Instead, his mind conjured up a girl with long, dark tresses and black, flashing eyes, her mysterious glance the last time he'd seen her. Marianela!

The kitchen door slammed. His father was up...a signal for Antonio to be out of bed. Immediately, he splashed himself with cold water from the pitcher and bowl on the washstand and combed his hair. The reflection of his young face in the mirror was striking: deep blue eyes, flecked with touches of green when the light was right, heavy lashes and eyebrows, sun-streaked, chestnut-colored hair— thick hair which waved slightly when damp from the comb. He touched the scar on his square chin. On first sight, it could have been mistaken for a cleft, but it was off-center, to the left and still slightly red, a deep scratch from a stick which flew up and hit him while he was cutting firewood. The scar didn't detract from the handsome face. His sister, Gloria, had said sympathetically, "It gives you a hint of...something romantic, Antonio. Makes you look a bit...worldly. Like you've been in a duel."

Antonio wasn't one to dawdle in front of the mirror; he drew on his clothes. At twenty, he was already taller than most men thereabout. Broad shouldered, muscular, he was also slender, slim of waist so that the work

9

trousers his mother sewed for him made pleats when he put on his belt. When he'd first tried them on, Dona Rosamaria laughed at her mistake. "I must have used the pattern for your father's trousers. I will take them in, Antonio. But as much as you eat, surely you'll fill them out soon!"

Antonio's room was furnished simply with handmade furniture. Besides the narrow bed, there were a small desk and chair, a washstand and a chest for his clothing. The adobe walls were whitewashed, the ceiling made of long vigas crossed with cedar latillas above. In one corner of the room was a small fireplace, seldom used except in winter; in the opposite corner was a niche for his patron saint, St. Joseph. On the wall between the window and the door hung three heirlooms once belonging to Antonio's great-grandfathers: There were a black, broad-brimmed hat made of stiff felt (stenciled on the lining were the name and address of the maker in Madrid, Spain), a pair of silver spurs and a riding crop made of finely woven horsehair. Antonio's father, Don Miguel Ortiz, had entrusted these keepsakes to him.

But to the casual observer, the most remarkable feature in his room was a number of clumps—perhaps they resembled bouquets?—of carefully tied herbs and plants hanging from the vigas. They were the collection which Antonio had studiously and methodically made over the past few years. They, too, were his prized possessions.

Before he left his room, Antonio knelt devoutly and prayed before St. Joseph. Then, outside his door, he lifted his head to the wide expanse of sky. The sun's first rays were touching the highest puffy clouds, setting them aglow in pastel pink and saffron. Soon a deep crimson would flood the land, turn to orange, then—the warming sun. The pageantry of the color never failed to hypnotize him. The magic of those few moments always held him spellbound.

The bent, familiar form of old Alfredo, one of Miguel's shepherds, hobbled down the road toward the sheep pens. Antonio greeted him. "Buenos días, le de Dios, Alfredo!"

The shepherd's faint, wheezing answer came back, "Gracias, y Dios le de un día igual, Antonio!"

Remembering his brother in the next room, Antonio knocked on his door. "Francisco, get up! Are you awake?" The sleepy answer, "Uuh!" was enough to make Antonio rap again. "Get up! You're sleeping your life away. You're missing everything...including breakfast!"

Dona Josefa came from around the corner of her house across the road carrying a pail. "Buenos días, madrina!" Antonio greeted his godmother.

"You're watering early."

"Morning is the best time. It's going to be a warm day and I must keep my plants alive. There's been so little rain this year."

Noting the profusion of forsythia and daffodils in bloom along her rock wall, Antonio commented, "Yellow seems to be the color of spring."

"Don't overlook my bluebells and violas." The old woman's face creased with pride as she smiled and pointed to the little bed of flowers she watered. "But just look at those rosas de Castilla! With the sunshine on them, don't they remind you of lemon snowballs?"

Antonio laughed. "I don't know. I never saw lemon snowballs."

Then Comadre Juanita called from her yard, "Buenos días, Josefa! Antonio!" Juanita was drawing water to start her family's breakfast.

"I'm going to pick the rosebuds today, Juanita. Do you want some?" Josefa called to her neighbor.

"I will appreciate them," Juanita replied as she looked at the clouds ascending over the mountains to the west. "Looks like rain today!"

"We could use it. I'd welcome a downpour. But I must water my flowers in case it doesn't rain."

As Juanita walked into her small, two-room adobe, Antonio asked Josefa, "Is the bud of the Castillian rose really good for fevers and sore throats?"

"I've always used them. So did my mother and grandmother. Your mother swears by them—gave them to you children when you were sick. The trick is in knowing how to make the tea from them. I will show you some day." Josefa had instructed Antonio with her knowledge of medicinal plants and herbs for as long as he could remember. She'd shown him where certain plants and herbs grew, when to pick them and their uses. But at that moment, he didn't linger to talk for he heard his father in the courtyard and went to greet him.

"Buenos días, papa!"

"God has given us another glorious day, my son. Is your brother up?" Don Miguel asked.

"I woke him just now."

"Good. And what are you going to do today?"

"I'd like to finish the corral for Chula."

"Fine. I hope you can. We must prepare for lambing the next day or so. I'll need you," Don Miguel said as they walked together toward the kitchen.

11

The resemblance between the two was striking. Antonio was a slightly taller, more slender copy of Miguel. Their carriage and stride were the same. At the door, Antonio held it for his father and made a sweeping, playful bow. "After you, señor!"

"Gracias, mi capitán!" Although there was no hint of trouble in Miguel's voice as he answered Antonio in the play, Antonio noted a worried look on his father's face. Miguel was a rugged man. His face was lined from being out of doors each eay in the searing sun and wind, but now Antonio noticed a new worry line on Miguel's brow.

"What is it, father?" he asked. "You look troubled."

"Does it show so much? Ah Antonio!" Miguel sighed. "It's just this weather. We need rain. With so little snow this winter, I fear for our stock. If it doesn't rain soon—and plentifully—we must reduce our herds drastically. That may not mean so much hardship for our family. We can survive. But I worry about my men. They need their work. Well, that's a rancher's life. Always the weather!" He clapped his son on the shoulder in a reassuring manner. "But let's not worry your mother. No need for her to fret. Come, she'll be waiting breakfast." Don Miguel's caution was needless for his wife was a most sensitive woman, finely tuned to her husband's every care.

Dona Rosamaria stood at the kitchen window, waiting. Antonio greeted her with a kiss. She looked up at the clock over the mantle and with a tone of exasperation said, "If you'd been a few minutes later, we could call this lunch." Then she sat calmly at her long, oval, oak table and poured coffee. The platters of food were already there to be served.

As the three bowed their heads, Don Miguel prayed, "We thank Thee for this food, oh Lord!. We use it for Thy eternal Glory. Amen."

In her soft, musical voice, Dona Rosamaria added, "And if it pleases You, dear God...send rain today."

Miguel and Antonio looked up at her in surprise. The expression on Dona Rosamaria's exquisite face was solemn. Her wide-set, blue eyes met Miguel's in a clear gaze as he looked at the woman he adored—but constantly amazed him. She pretended ignorance at his surprise as she also pretended to complain: "This bread! I don't know why it didn't rise so well yesterday." Then she heaped their plates saying, "I let the girls sleep late this morning. But where is Francisco, Antonio?"

"I woke him, mama."

As she watched Antonio finish his second helping, she asked, "Would you please wake him again, Antonio? I don't have time to serve three breakfasts this morning. We're finishing carding the wool today."

"I'll get him up!" Antonio answered as he gulped the last of his coffee. "May I be excused?" With his parents' nod of approval, he left the room muttering—outside the door—"I'm not his nursemaid."

Antonio rapped on Francisco's door. It opened and the sleepy brother emerged. "It's about time," Antonio admonished.

"Why the scowl?"

"Mother's waiting breakfast for you and father wants you to go with him," Antonio replied curtly. "And I'm tired of having to see you're up. You're...grown! Not a child!"

"But you're my big brother," Francisco teased the way he knew would rankle Antonio.

Antonio hurried to the corral he was building for his mare, Chula. She had foaled two days before and needed a place of her own. While he nailed the boards, he heard his father and brother ride out. He hadn't been working long when he was interrupted by a deep, booming voice greeting him.

The commanding figure on horseback was a familiar one to Antonio. Don Crescencio was a powerfully built man with burly, thick neck and shoulders. His head seemed larger than most men's and so were his expressive eyes which shone with a light of their own. He wore a wide-brimmed sombrero with a tall crown, a great leather coat, his rawhide chaps flapped over his thick legs. It was only when he dismounted one realized he was short and overweight because the sweeping impression was of his wind and sun weathered face, his full head of hair and flowing moustache and the rich timbre of his bass voice—a voice like no other in the entire countryside.

"Buenos días, Don Crescencio! I didn't hear you ride up."

Don Crescencio offered a broad smile, "You were too busy hammering."

"How are you, señor?"

"Fine—except for these twinges in my joints. He shifted uncomfortably in his saddle.

"And Dona Thomasita?"

"She is well. Thank you!"

Antonio asked about Crecencio's two sons and three daughters. He carefully mentioned Marianela last, stammering when he spoke the name of the girl who was so much on his mind, especially since this was her father.

Don Crescencio laughed. "That little dove? I can't for the life of me imagine what's got into her of late. She daydreams most of the time. When I ask my wife what is the matter, Dona Thomasita smiles and says, 'Oh, it's nothing. She'll get over it by and by.' But otherwise, Marianela is well, thank you!"

Antonio felt his heart beat fast. A lump came in his throat. He hoped the older man would not notice this feeling and after an awkward silence, he said, "Father rode out to Pelón to see about some sheep."

"But, it's you I've come to see, Antonio."

"Me?" Antonio was taken aback.

"Yes. For a young man, you have quite a reputation as a trainer of horses—the best I am told."

"Thank you, Don Crescencio!"

"I would like you to do a favor for me, if you will—and if your father can spare your time. I want you to break a filly for me. She's one from my herd. And I would like for you to do it here in the village—as secretly as possible."

Again, with surprise, Antonio answered, "I don't know how secretly it's possible...the village is small...everyone knows everyone else's business."

"Well, the village people don't need to know who owns the horse." Crecencio's voice lowered to a whisper, which still could be heard at some distance. "That will be secret enough."

"Fair enough. I'll certainly try to do this for you."

"You may wonder at my request, but there is a reason. You see, Marianela has had her eye on this filly for some time and I would like to present it to her for her coming birthday."

Antonio swelled with pride. "Then it will be more than a pleasure—it will be an honor, Don Crescencio. If you will have the horse delivered to me, I shall do my best to prepare your daughter a well-trained riding mare in time for her birthday."

"Gracias, Antonio! I know you will do so with utmost care and attention. You are gentle and you care for animals. I like the horses you have trained for yourself and your family." Then with a glance toward the southwest, he indicated the massing clouds. "Give your parents my best regards. Tell Miguel I will ride over to see him before lambing. Now I must be on my way before the rainstorm; I feel it in my bones we are going to have a good one today," he said, slapping his arthritic knee and then he was off, leaving Antonio with hammer in hand, mouth slightly agape, dazed from the encounter.

With Marianela's father out of earshot, Antonio could no longer contain his elation—he threw up his arms and jumped in the air. He let out a whoop. "Whooooeee!" Then he executed a few steps of a dance of joy. His mind leaped to the time he would lead the prized filly he'd trained to the Salas hacienda. He saw Marianela's face. *She'll really be surprised...her eyes will sparkle...she'll be so excited she'll throw her arms around me and...her lips...like delicate rosebuds...soft as pink petals!*

With his initial moment of exuberance spent, Antonio leaned on the corral, looking into the distance, dreaming. He saw Marianela walking toward him, her slim form floating, elegant and noble, her long, black hair loose, caressing her face, strands touching her tiny waist. Standing with a handful of square nails in one hand, his hammer in the other, he laughed aloud, so caught up in his thoughts he didn't hear his father's footsteps. Don Miguel startled him.

"Hijo, what is so funny you laugh to yourself?"

"Papa! I didn't hear you. I was daydreaming, I suppose. And I shouldn't be for I haven't finished this corral. Have you already been to Pelón?"

"Francisco and I decided to return. There's too much danger from lightning to ride this morning. As I rode back, I thought I saw Crescencio riding away. Did he wish to see me?"

"He asked me to pay his respects to you. He was in a hurry to be back at his ranch before the rain."

"What did he want?"

"Actually he came to see me, papa." Antonio couldn't conceal his delight as he told Miguel of Crecencio's request.

"I see! I see!" Miguel was both pleased and amused as he watched his son's face; now he understood Antonio's preoccupation. "Crescencio is a shrewd and clever man...in many ways. I'm certain he will surprise and please his fine daughter," he said knowingly. "But, Antonio, have you noticed anything different about yourself lately?"

"Why, no, father! What do you mean? I'm the same..."

"You've grown. I do believe you are at least ten feet tall, my son."

"Oh, papa!"

"Well, it will be an exciting job for you and I know it will be most rewarding," Miguel said with a grin. "By the way, have you spoken with Marianela recently?"

"I haven't seen her since the rodeo at Don Crescencio's and then, only briefly. If you remember, those calves of his we branded kept us busy. I barely had a chance to speak to her when we broke for lunch."

"I noticed the way she looked at you that day," Miguel said looking at his son, sizing him. "I think it is time you and she know each other better, Antonio." He paused, adding a word of caution, "Before too long!" With that bidding, which his son understood was both permission and warning, Miguel turned his attention to other matters. "Your corral is almost finished …maybe in another hour? But first, would you help me apply some salve on that bull's injured leg?"

"Of course, papa." As the two went to the pen, Antonio couldn't remember when he felt happier. Uppermost in his mind was Crescencio's request. *I'll see her more often, surely. And father gave me permission to call on her,* he thought reassuringly. To his father he said, "What's in that salve Martina prepared? I can't believe it's healing so quickly. I thought we'd have to butcher him."

Miguel answered, "Martina doesn't like to divulge her secrets but she has no equal in her knowledge of herbs, especially in the making of poltices. I marvel at her skill."

Don Miguel and Antonio had just finished ministering to the crippled bull when a bright bolt of lightning streaked the sky overhead followed in seconds by cracking thunder. "The storm's here at last!" Miguel said as the first drops of rain fell on them. Dona Rosamaria came out to assess the weather with them and she looked up at the piles of black clouds with a smile on her lips. Miguel came up to her, put an arm about her and murmured, "Now this earth will be blessed." It was almost a prayer. Then the three hurried into the kitchen.

The kitchen was the room of the Ortiz hacienda everyone enjoyed most; it radiated a closeness—the intimacy of uninterrupted years of family life. The ceilings were a bit lower in the kitchen wing of the house because they were the first built. In one end of the room was a large fireplace with a spit and iron pots for cooking. The fireplace had served mistresses of the house for two centuries. On the mantle, on either side of the clock, were figurines and vases of porcelain brought from Europe. To one side of the fireplace was a shelf on which the lady of the house kept her spices, herbs and special condiments while on the other side stood a trastero in which she kept dishes. Dona Rosamaria kept her best china in the dining room. Along the walls were storage boxes for flour, lard and sugar. Strings of chili hung from vigas, as did dried beef, wrapped in sacks. The table with its white cloth was surrounded by sturdy chairs. A meticulous housekeeper, Rosamaria ran her household with an ableness matching Miguel's in ranching.

As his wife poured coffee, Miguel marveled at her composure and loveliness. At forty, Rosamaria kept her figure, her hair hadn't grayed. She was still the petite blonde Miguel had fallen in love with and married.

Dona Rosamaria retained the disciplines of her youth. Each morning she rose one hour before anyone else in the house—including Miguel. She used that early time for meditation, prayers and making her toilette. Her family, at breakfast, was accustomed to the sight of her dressed in a fresh frock, hair carefully braided into a knot at the nape of her graceful neck, curls framing her face. Her smile and ability to converse were as welcoming as the food she prepared. No matter how long and arduous her chores of the day, Rosamaria's manner was unruffled and easy which gave the impression she'd just stepped out of her dressing room. First-time visitors to the hacienda were surprised to encounter such a lady in that remote place.

"Listen to that beautiful, beautiful rain!" Rosamaria said as she brought her cup to the table and sat beside her husband.

Miguel took her hand in his and smiled. "There will be grass. Work for everyone. God has been good to us."

Rosamaria showed a slight expression of concern. Her husband asked, "What is it, my dear?"

"Nothing really. I was just thinking of the visita this coming Saturday night at the Salas hacienda."

"Is it this week? We must prepare for lambing this week." Miguel said.

"I hope the roads aren't so muddy that they will spoil Dona Thomasita's party," Rosamaria added.

Antonio hadn't forgotten they were going to Marianela's house. The visita was very much on his mind—just like Marianela. He seldom spent an hour without thinking of her. *Someday I hope to marry her and be as happy as my mother and father,* he thought, seeing them sitting side by side holding hands. The idea of them having been young once came to his mind and, to his parents' amusement, he suddenly asked, "...Where did you two meet? How did you get to know each other?"

Miguel laughed and turned to his wife. There was a slight blush on her cheeks. Miguel teased, "Why shouldn't we tell our eldest child about our courtship? After all, he's grown...he'll be married soon himself."

"If you wish," Rosamaria answered with a coquettish glance.

Miguel cleared his throat as if starting to tell a serious story. "I met your mother at a ball given in her honor at Santa Fe. My family was invited by her family."

"It was all very proper," Rosamaria added.

"And after I saw her, I was never to look—or think about—another woman!" Miguel flashed his beguiling smile.

"But I had a lot of suitors, remember?"

"That you did. But you told me you had eyes only for me."

"And my heart!"

Miguel squeezed her hand, then turned to Antonio. "But courting your mother wasn't easy. Her parents lived at Cañon Blanco...quite a ride for me. I didn't get to see her too often."

"Then there was mother!" Rosamaria reminded. "My mother was quite ambitious for me. She didn't want me to marry a rancher."

"And your father was a merchant," Miguel said.

"Yes, but mother always had her way. That's why I was sent to the convent. She wanted me to be educated. I remember my parents quarelling. Mama said 'I want her to have every opportunity to be a lady if she chooses. Not just a rancher's wife.' Papa said, 'Has your life here with me been so terrible?' To which mama replied, 'You know I love you. I'd choose to marry you again—if it were to be done over. But we have money, and I want her to have every chance we can give her.'" Rosamaria drew a deep breath. "That was the beginning of three long years of studying. Papa kept insisting after I left for the convent I'd marry a rancher. He said, 'With that girl's love of this country—and horses!—she'll never leave here.'" Rosamaria patted Miguel's arm affectionately. "And papa was right. Although I've no time for horses anymore."

"So, after the ball where did you meet...?" Antonio urged.

"We fell in love at the ball, didn't we?" Miguel said looking deep into Rosamaria's eyes.

"Yes." Turning to her son, she said, "But mama wasn't pleased. There were scenes. She'd cry when I told her I wished to marry Miguel. 'You'd have *him*? Marry a rancher, live a life of hardship in that dusty little village of San Lucas?' I reminded her, 'Why not? You married a rancher and live at Cañon Blanco.' That brought more tears. She said, 'Your father was right all along. Well, I've tried. I've seen you've had the best we could offer.

Now...if you wish to throw it all away...'"

"And that was that?" Antonio asked.

"Well, it all took time, of course. When I announced my intention, my parents called on hers and formally asked for her hand in marriage. Then we went through the proper customs...and her mother's tears. But, in the end, we were married!" Miguel put his arm around his wife, kissed her on the forehead. Then, to Antonio, with a big smile, "And that was that! You'll see how it is. Now, rain or no, we've work to do. We can't sit here in the kitchen all day talking about...love."

Antonio wasn't the only one excited about the approaching party. A few miles away at the Salas hacienda, Marianela and her sisters were in their room. Marianela brushed her hair while Rafaela sewed and Ofelia finished some needlework.

"This thread! It's knotted again," Rafaela exclaimed.

"You'll never finish that skirt in time for the visita," Ofelia chided.

"It seems so long until Saturday," Marianela lamented. "I can't wait to see ...everyone."

"Especially Antonio!" Rafaela said with a giggle.

"Why is he so shy? We've known each other all our lives. Why is it now we don't seem to be able to talk easily as we did when we were children?"

"Maybe you're afraid you'll show the feelings you have for each other?" suggested Ofelia knowingly.

"How do I know what his feelings are? He never tells me. I'm not a mind reader." Marianela snapped.

"And what are your feelings for him?"

"I'm certainly not going to tell you two!"

"You don't have to. It's written on your face when he's around."

At the appointed hour of six that Saturday night, the invited families arrived. The women, dressed in finery of satins, silks and lace, were escorted by their handsomely attired men as they drove through the well-lighted puertón. Grooms took the carriages and horses, then directed the guests to the sala de recibo where Don Crescencio and his family awaited.

The sala was large and reflected the family's wealth. Tapestries and paintings adorned the walls. Glowing candelabras and colorful lamps lit the darkest corners of the room. Dona Thomasita had spread a feast on a long, banquet table at one end. Two guitarists played in the background. Their sala was always a welcome sight for their guests.

As he entered with his family—fortified by Don Crescencio's recent request and his own father's permission—Antonio went directly to Marianela. His chest tightened as he caught sight of her *She's even lovelier than when I last saw her! I must tell her so,* he thought. There was so much he wanted to say that moment but he had that helpless feeling again and heard himself say only, "It's good to see you, Marianela."

"Thank you, Antonio! You're practically a stranger. I haven't seen you for so long. Don't you pass this way anymore when you ride to your father's rancho?"

"I do most of the time. But it's such an early or late hour I always think you must be asleep or busy when I pass with the vaqueros."

"Well, news of you does come our way. I heard you've a new colt."

"Chula had a splendid colt. You've seen me ride Chula?"

"Someday I'd like to have a mare as fine as she." For an awkward moment neither could think what to say. Then, with a merry twinkle in her eye, Marianela remembered some gossip. "I hear from the villagers you're becoming very involved in studying healing herbs. And...writing! Is it true?"

Taken aback by her knowledge of his endeavors and her interest in him, Antonio blushed and faltered. "It's...true. Sometimes my fascination with the world of healing herbs surprises me. There's no end to what one can learn."

And the writing? What sorts of things do you write?"

"Mostly poems."

"Oh? About...?"

His cheeks burned. "They are poems...in honor of God's mighty plants," he replied. *How can I tell her I write about love...poems about how I feel toward her?* he thought.

"I think that's wonderful. I don't know how you find time to study and write with all the ranch work you do. But, Antonio! You may not believe me, but I, too, am interested in plants and herbs. I haven't started to learn as much about them as I'd like. Why, only the other day, the old bruja, La Concha, stopped by for a moment. Mother asked her to leave some herbs to sprinkle around the hacienda to ward off evil spirits. I was intrigued by how much La Concha knows about herbs...and her positive attitude. She seems to fear no one, either good or evil."

It didn't matter to Antonio if Marianela jumped from one subject to another. He was only interested in being with the girl he loved. Taking her lead, he offered, "If you'd like, maybe you could join me on a walk some morning...perhaps next week? I'll be glad to share what little I know about medicinal plants." His new-found bravery and the prospect of being with her made his pulse race.

"I'll ask mother...to speak to father." Marianela was aglow with excitement. "I'm sure he'll say yes. Mother will probably let either Rafaela or Ofelia accompany us."

Just then, Dona Rosamaria came up to them. "I wanted to tell you how lovely you look tonight, Marianela. Your new gown is exquisite. White becomes you, don't you agree Antonio?"

"Yes. I certainly do, mama!" Antonio said, wishing he'd said the words his mother spoke. *Why can't I tell her 'Marianela, you bewitch me. Your face is like a rare portrait. You're beautiful.'*

These ranching families enjoyed the get-togethers in each other's homes. It was timeout from their work lives; a chance for the men to gather in groups and discuss everyday problems, the women to cluster and exchange bits of gossip. Of course, the young took the opportunity to play and flirt, but always under the watchful eyes of their parents. After dinner, it was the custom for the host to request a story. One of the older guests was usually selected to tell it. That evening Don Crescencio asked, "Señor Chavez! Would you honor us with one of your famous cuentos?"

The old man accepted graciously and a chair was placed in the center of the room for him. As everyone settled around him, Señor Chavez began a story about two lovers:

The Gringo with the Golden Earring

This is a story that happened many, many years ago in a small, remote village, high in the mountains of northern New Mexico, where the people were descendants of early Spanish settlers. And, of course, there were Indians living in the nearby pueblos. The people of the village raised sheep and made a few crops and gardens. Life was not easy and the villagers had little time for social life. A special event for them was the arrival of a wagontrain which came about once a year. Now the village was not on the main route the gringo traders usually took from the eastern United States through Missouri and across the Santa Fe Trail, yet once in a great while a group of traders would pull off the Trail and visit the village to peddle wares.

Trading was brisk and honesty prevailed between villagers and traders because of their mutual respect. But there was more than buying and selling, for the villagers enjoyed mingling with these strange, fair-skinned men—many of whom had blue eyes. The arrival of the wagontrain became a grand event, for after a hard day of trading a fandango was held in the evening. There was food and drink aplenty for guests and hosts alike. The revelry went on into the early morning hours before the feasting and dancing stopped.

On one evening after such a day of trading, there was a tall, blonde haired, young gringo who rode in with the wagons. His eyes were the blue of the sky, his skin tanned the color of burnished copper and he wore in his right ear a small, golden earring. Some at the dance whispered, "He may be a pirate!" That evening, he spent the greater part of his time dancing with one of the village's most beautiful young señoritas. His attention caused her parents some anxiety. They kept a careful watch over their daughter and the gringo but, at the same time, felt honored this striking man found their daughter so attractive. In the crowd of villagers there were, of course, young men who did not appreciate the presence of this gringo, for they also had eyes for the señorita. Even so, there was no fighting and nothing was said, for everyone knew the caravan would move on in the morning.

The wagon train did leave the next morning at sun-up. Many of the villages were out to see it off, as was the custom. Among them was the señorita, waving goodbye to the handsome young man with the golden earring.

Señor Chavez stopped a moment to sip his drink; the girls listening to him sighed and the young men stirred uneasily in their chairs.

Years went by, but one day that young gringo returned. This time he rode into the village alone. On his arrival, he went directly to the home of the señorita and inquired about her. To his delight and surprise, her parents told him she remained at home, as yet unmarried. She had waited for his promised return. In time, they were married and three children were born to them. He was the first gringo to live in the village.

The couple lived happily until one day a great tragedy occurred. An epidemic of smallpox or perhaps it was cholera hit the village.

Many died. The church bells tolled constantly. The lovely wife of the gringo was one who was stricken and died.

There was great sadness and sorrow for Death took loved ones from every home. The gringo grieved deeply and became very depressed. In time, he felt unable to take care of his three young children and their grandparents told him they would raise them. Even so, his despondency reached such depths he told his wife's parents he wished to leave the village.

"But where will you go?" they asked. "Your life is here with us."

"I will go in search of my love," he replied.

At first they did not understand him but then it became clear he meant to look for his wife. "But, son! She is dead," they told him.

He would not hear them. "I will find her. I must!" he insisted.

Nothing they said could dissuade him and eventually he sold his possessions and bade them goodbye, saying, "My life here has been shattered. I must find my beautiful wife. I will look for her in all the valleys and in all the forests. I will search the mountains, the mesas. I will look everywhere and I will find her." Before he departed on his quest, he told a gathering, "I leave all young lovers a gift—but only to those who want true and lasting love, to those who will love and want to be loved in return. This gift will be theirs only when they find me in this valley, for part of me will always remain here and this part will grant young lovers their dreams and wishes." With those mysterious words he disappeared.

Years have gone by. Yet, when young men and women of the village walk hand in hand over the hills, down in the valleys and back into the groves of piñon and sit under the shelter of rocks, their excuse is they are looking for the gringo.

There were twitters of laughter from the young people. Dona Thomasita clucked, "And their parents would not approve of their excuse...looking for a gringo, indeed!"

Señor Chavez went on:

But the story is not as strange as it may seem because—time after time, even today—those who truly love each other and search for that gringo have found him. They see him in a quiet, lonely place when they least expect. They may be walking along, talking about their futures or sitting by a rippling stream when, all of a sudden they look up and see a faint outline of a person—a tall, blonde haired young man wearing a golden earring. They all report he is dressed in a garb of white. When they see that apparition, the couples tell they feel a complete belonging to one another.

He continued:

But that is not all. The lovers not only see the gringo but also hear him say in a clear, quiet voice these words:

The night nor the day wishes to be for you and me,
So let our love live in our own world made of
Dreams and memory.
I wear this earring, my love the other.

Then he disappears!

Señor Chavez' audience sat spellbound, waiting. As he looked at Antonio and Marianela who sat close to each other holding hands, he smiled at them. "I'm sure if you really want to find him, he will be there waiting for you."

The story told, the hour late, the guests bade their hosts goodnight. As he left, Antonio reminded Marianela, "Let me know if I can come for you next week?"

"I'll send word soon," she answered as they parted.

The moon showed the way as Antonio and his family rode home. Antonio thought only of Marianela. *Her hand is so soft and warm. Did I feel her tremble as we touched? When Señor Chavez told the story about the gringo's gift, didn't her hand tell me we belong together?*

After the horses were stabled, the family stood on their front porch admiring the moon.

Seeing his son stare only at his feet, Don Miguel nudged his wife, "Aren't you well, Antonio?"

But Antonio only excused himself and, as if in a dream, he said goodnight and went to his room—the aroma of Marianela's perfume haunting him to his pillow, taunting him to sleep.

Three days after the visita, Antonio and Francisco rode out to see about some stray cattle. As they returned to the village, Antonio noticed someone picking fruit from Dona Josefa's trees. "Isn't that Marianela?" he called.

"You're just wishing," Francisco replied.

"It is! And her sisters. They're picking apricots."

The young men rode up to the girls; Marianela made a wry face. When she saw Antonio grinning at her, she threw away the green apple she was eating. "I must look ridiculous," she said. "Eating a green apple..."

Antonio laughed. "Why don't you eat the ripe apricots?"

"Mother brought us here this morning," she said vaguely.

"Have you asked your parents?" he whispered.

"I did, but father hasn't given his consent yet. I'll let you know as soon..."

Just then Dona Thomasita called, "Hurry girls! We must be going home shortly. Don't dawdle!"

The girls took the baskets of apricots inside. "She smiles at you real sweet-like!" Francisco teased and spurred his horse, leaving Antonio in a cloud of dust.

That Friday, Antonio was working in the blacksmith shop at the hacienda making Chula new shoes when he was interrupted by the hunchback Pedro, a servant of Don Crescencio's.

"Buenas tardes, Señor Antonio! Marianela has sent me with a message," the little fellow said.

"Gracias, Pedro!"

"She said to tell you she will be ready to ride with you tomorrow morning. She would like to start as early as possible. Let me know if you can come."

Antonio's quick smile was answer enough but he replied, "Tell her I'll be there before sunrise. I'm grateful for your bringing me the message, Pedro."

The deformed man lurched away in his peculiar gait and Antonio thought, *Dear God, I marvel at your creations! Pedro—with all his deformities—is never known to frown.*

Antonio was up even earlier than his mother the next morning. He saddled Chula and was off—Morro, the foal, trotted closely behind her mother. Two questions were uppermost in his mind: did Marianela have the same feelings for him as he had for her? And, when would Don Crescencio send that filly? Daydreaming, he was in the Salas' courtyard before he knew it. The Don was there to greet him.

"I understand Marianela and Ofelia are going with you to search for herbs this morning," Don Crescencio said with a pleased smile. "Well, good hunting! This land abounds in them. And, Antonio, I'll have that filly delivered next week."

Just then, the two young ladies appeared. Marianela, dressed in a mulberry colored riding dress, her braided hair fastened with a turquoise-studded, silver hairpin. Her cheeks were flushed with excitement. Antonio's heart filled with pride. He turned to the Don. "I'm grateful for your permission to escort your daughters, Don Crescencio. You may be assured I'll be most responsible for them." Only one thing would have pleased Antonio more—to be alone with Marianela, but such things never happened. Yet he knew Ofelia would be understanding and give them their moments to be alone.

"Have a good ride and be careful!" Don Crescencio called as they left.

The sun was starting to peek over the horizon. "What a sunrise! I seldom see it," Marianela said.

"But you sit and sigh, watching a lot of sunsets," Ofelia teased.

"I should get up earlier," Marianela said, ignoring her sister's taunt. "Each new day is like being born again, isn't it, Antonio?"

"A new life," he answered, looking at her with adoration in his eyes.

"You two!" Ofelia chided. "If you're going to be so profound, I'm riding ahead."

For a few embarrassed moments they said nothing. Then Antonio continued. "Many of the plants and flowers are reborn every day."

"Oh?"

"Many bloom at night. The evening primrose unfolds its petals just as the sun goes down. The blossom is full when the sun's first rays touch them in the morning."

"I didn't know that."

His mind only on her, *She's like a flower, herself.*

They came to a box canyon where the vegetation was lush. "Why don't we stop awhile?" Marianela suggested. Ofelia returned and the three staked their horses and walked, Ofelia lagging tactfully behind. Antonio picked some brilliant red blooms of Indian paintbrush. He held them up to Marianela. "The color of your lips puts this flower to shame," he said boldly.

"So what can the flor de Santa Rita do for us?" Marianela asked accusingly, trying to hide her feelings.

"It makes your face light up with a lovely radiance," he said and he gave her the flowers and took her hand and they walked together.

He's strong and warm, Marianela thought. *I feel safe...secure with him.* She'd never walked hand in hand with a man before.

My heart's beating so fast, I wonder if he can hear it pounding?''

Antonio was excited. *She let me take her hand without a protest. She clings to me. She must feel toward me as I feel toward her.* He looked down at her and squeezed her hand; she looked up at him, her eyes dancing with excitement and together they almost stumbled over a hedgehog cactus. They broke into peals of laughter, their eyes meeting in the sheer delight of their mutual mistake. It was a moment of recognition and, with Ofelia keeping a respectful distance, they wandered on, deliriously happy.

They stopped at the bank of a stream and sat on a huge boulder listening to the water curl at their feet. Ofelia joined them. "Oh, let's go wading."

"Why not?"

"That cold water'll feel good. Here, let me help you with your boots," Antonio offered.

Marianela modestly raised her riding skirt, exposing her boots. Antonio felt clumsy as he straddled her foot and pulled. The boot came off easily and fast and he fell backward and landed with a splash, boot in hand.

After the initial moment of surprise, the girls broke into hysterical laughter. "Oh, Antonio! You're so...wet!" Ofelia howled.

"I guess I'll have to dry out!" he said, sitting upright in the water trying to smile but still too stunned to laugh.

After an hour in the sun they returned to the horses and rode until midday when they stopped to eat lunch under a tall pine. The girls unwrapped the pack of food Dona Thomasita had given them. Ofelia took her lunch and sat under a tree a few yards away.

"I love to hear you laugh—even if it is at me," Antonio said unabashedly.

"It's been a grand day. I wish it could go on and on and on."

"Can we do this again...soon?"

"I hope so. I'll ask. But I don't know if Ofelia has had much fun. I'll ask Rafaela next time. She can be our shadow." Laughing at the joke, Marianela added, "I'm lucky to have such nice sisters."

"They're lucky to have you," Antonio said and took her hand in his.

"We must be going home, Antonio. It's a long ride back. I promised mother..."

"I've never spent such a wonderful day. I've been so happy..."

"And you had a free bath!"

"I must've looked like a wet dog."

"A very surprised one!"

Shortly after, the three turned their horses toward home. More clouds were building in the southwest. They hurried to arrive ahead of the squall.

Antonio remained at the Salas hacienda a few hours, visiting with the family as he waited for the rain to stop. The trio of herb-hunters recounted the day's events, bringing rounds of laughter when they described Antonio's bath. Seeing how delighted Marianela was as she talked—her voice was light with laughter—her parents knew precisely how she felt toward Antonio.

When the exhausted but elated Antonio arrived home, his mother greeted him and inquired about his day. "Change, then I'll fix you a cup of hot yerba buena tea." Then she sat with him in the kitchen and listened. The two had always felt a special closeness and Dona Rosamaria now knew her own feelings were to be shared by another.

Don Miguel's comment was—"Is that what you call a day's work? Where are the herbs you gathered, Antonio?"

"I'm afraid we didn't pick any, father."

"I don't know if I approve of the way you go about gathering herbs. I hope you don't decide to become a curandero. What's a curandero without herbs? You'd better decide to be a patrón."

"Can't I be both? After all, the two professions deal with the welfare of the people."

Don Miguel didn't pursue the subject. For the first time he sensed how serious his son felt about his life. The boy—who was no longer a boy—wasn't kidding. Neither would he.

Within a few days, Don Crescencio had the young filly delivered. "What a great sorrel! Look at the pretty white blaze on her face—and her three white stockings," Antonio exclaimed.

"Marianela's named her Cara Linda," the vaquero who brought her said.

"She bewitches me...like her mistress," Antonio said beneath his breath.

"You have your work cut out," the vaquero warned. "She's high-spirited and already has some bad habits she's learned from the herd she's been running with."

Antonio said confidently, "I'll start training her today. In a month, Cara Linda will be ready for Marianela."

One cloudy, rainy day after the men left the breakfast table, Dona Thomasita marshalled her daughters and Emma, a servant woman who'd been with the family for over twenty years, "We must jerk the beef Crescencio butchered today," she advised. "And start cleaning house."

"What about the apples?" Emma asked.

"We'll peel them and get them ready to dry this afternoon."

"That's too much to do in one day," Ofelia complained.

"Are we to wait until the beef spoils and the apples rot?" her mother said smiling and lifting the girl's face to hers. "We'll survive, dear. You may have your merienda this afternoon. I've made some special cookies for you."

At midday as they were washing dishes after lunch, Marianela asked, "Don't you ever tire of doing the same thing day in and day out, mama?"

"What a question."

"There are always so many things to do...over and over."

"Like cooking, washing, preparing food, getting ready for winter? That's life on a rancho, but I take pride in what we women accomplish. I suppose it has never occurred to me to have any other life."

"But don't you ever want to do...something different?"

"Each day is different in its way. People are different...never the same. When you're married and have your own family, you'll know what I mean."

In the afternoon, the girls sat under the back portal, peeling and slicing apples. One of the girls' favorite pastimes while they worked was baiting Emma. "Have you seen Manuel Garcia lately? Isn't he getting handsome?"

"He's not as good looking as Juan Chavez!" Ofelia chimed.

Statements such as these riled Emma who, at forty, was a spinster and had never had a good word for any man except her patrón. Now she rose to the challenge. "Neither are what I call handsome. I hear bad things about each." Then she launched into a tirade, belittling the young men without knowing them and finishing with: "I advise you girls to have nothing to do with them." Emma believed her generous moral advice kept the sisters from the paths of degradation.

Marianela said, "Antonio is certainly comely—you haven't heard anything bad about him!"

Emma answered, "Here we are, trying to finish these bushels of apples to set out in the sun, if it ever decides to shine again, and all you young ladies talk about is men!"

"But Emma! Antonio is not just another man. You've known him since he was born. You've watched him grow to manhood."

"Men! They'll only break your heart. They never tell the truth."

"He's from a very good family," Rafaela suggested.

"Don't you think he's an odd one?" Emma snapped, "with all his father's lands and sheep, he wants to be a curandero. Why, he practically worships weeds!"

"I won't hear any more of this nonsense, Emma. You don't trust anyone." Marianela was furious.

"I trust your father," Emma replied haughtily, pursing her narrow lips.

Ofelia deliberately changed the conversation. "When are we going to make plans for Marianela's birthday celebration, mama?"

"I wish we could have a fandango for my birthday," Marianela begged. "Could father get the musicians from San Lucas? That family plays best."

Not to be excluded from the planning, Emma, with a long martyrish sigh, said, "I'll have to help your poor mother with all that food and drink."

The three sisters went on excitedly with their plans for the dance but as they abandoned Emma to talk with their mother, Emma called icily, "And, of course, Marianela, all this dancing will give Antonio plenty of time to hold you in his arms and whisper..."

"You are terrible, Emma, but I love you anyway," Marianela laughed.

As Dona Thomasita listened to her daughters chirping away about the plans for the celebration, she nodded approvingly. "It's a month until Marianela's birthday, but I'll talk with your father about what you want. I'm sure he'll be agreeable. Besides, he and I haven't danced together for quite some time," she added with a twinkle in her eye. "Yes! I'd like to have a fandango."

Alone in her room, Marianela daydreamed of her birthday party and Antonio. *His eyes were all mine the day we rode through the countryside...will he look at me the same way at my party?...will he dance every dance he can with me? ...will he hold my hand the way he did?...will he hold me close...very close?... will he kiss me if he has the chance?...will he ever ask me to marry him?...I wish we could be together every day. I do care for him.*

Sunlight streamed through the window and fell on the red flowers Antonio had given her on their ride. Outside, a double rainbow made a twin arc over the distant hills. Marianela, moved by the sight, dipped her quill:

> *The wind softly strokes*
> *the rainbow, brings*
> *every color to its deepest.*
> *Stretching out, the rainbow*
> *creates a stairway to the sun.*
> *On the table your flowers*
> *blossom anew.*

"How I wish I could share this rainbow with Antonio," she sighed and folded the paper and put it away. "Maybe we could climb the stairway, hand in hand," she said wistfully.

One day not long after this while riding with Don Crescencio, Marianela saw his herd of remuda horses.

"Where's Cara Linda, papa?" she cried in alarm. "She's not with the herd."

"I forgot to tell you, my daughter. I had the vaqueros move her to another pasture a few days ago to be with a couple of other mares. I was afraid the stallion was beginning to eye her."

"Oh, papa! I want to train her. Cara Linda's such a smart horse. The way she runs in front of the herd makes me want to race her with the wind."

"I agree. She's grown well and about ready for training. Cara Linda will make you a fine horse."

Then he changed the subject to hide his secret. "Look at that patch of mastranzo! Your mother will want some to use for those winter colds that always plague us."

"Antonio pointed out some horehound to Ofelia and me the day we rode together. He said that herb has many uses besides colds. He said a bath made with it is good to treat frozen feet. And a gravy made with starch and mastranzo will cure stomach cramps."

Don Crescencio saw the animated glow on his daughter's face.

"Yes, that young man seems to be making quite a study of plants. I hadn't realized he was so interested, although Don Miguel did mention it once. So you're quite interested in Antonio?" he finished abruptly.

The quick blush in her cheeks confirmed his observation. He continued, "And I like Antonio. He is a fine young man, unafraid of work. And, his manner with horses impresses me."

"He's sensitive, papa. He has so much love for all God's creatures. I do care for him. And it makes me so happy to hear you say you like him. Thank you, papa!"

As they gathered the horehound and rode back to the hacienda, Marianela felt very close to her father. She thought how lucky she was for not every girl has an understanding father.

Antonio worked with Cara Linda every spare moment he had available. Completing a day's work on the rancho, he would rush through dinner so he could put in some extra time with the horse. "Aren't you tired, son? You've already done a day's work," his mother said.

"I don't feel tired, mama. It's something I want to do," he answered heading for the corral.

That night he saw one of his father's apple trees laden with fruit. The sight made him chuckle as he remembered what a silly face Marianela made when she ate that green apple. *But what a lovely face.* And, as usual, he felt a great need to express his feelings. It was his custom of late to write poetry. As he told Marianela later, "First I feel the poem in my heart. Finally it touches my soul and is born."

When he finished Cara Linda's evening training, he repaired to his desk and the lines sprang from his heart:

> *Marianela, everything belongs to her.*
> *White is her very own.*
> *The sunrise warms her.*
> *Apricots and apples like the touch of her hands.*
> *Unselfishly she gives.*
> *Her totalness is locked down deep past her soul,*
> *And only a taste of Marianela belongs to me.*
> *Plants and trees gently bow as she walks by,*
> *For her direction is respected.*
> *Some mystery remains, as I become richer*
> *When she passes my way.*

He read the poem aloud and vowed to gather the courage to give it to her as a birthday present. Then he rolled the paper and tied it with a red ribbon, placing it in one of his desk drawers.

Antonio began each day with a prayer he recited before an old, wooden

statue of St. Joseph holding the Christ Child. "Oh, St. Joseph, whose pro-
tection is so great, so strong, so prompt before the throne of God, I place in
you all my interests and desires. St. Joseph, do assist me by your powerful
intercession and obtain for me the blessing of your Divine Son. Press the
Child in your arms in my name and kiss His fine head and ask him to return
the kiss when I draw my dying breath. St. Joseph, pray for me."

It was a prayer Antonio's mother taught him when he was a small boy.
His day didn't seem to have a good beginning unless it started with the prayer.

After dressing, he walked from his room down the long stone walk to
the kitchen. His family was assembled for breakfast. The aroma from his
mother's kitchen made him hungrier. He greeted his parents with a kiss and
wished them good morning. His brother and sisters greeted Antonio politely.

"It's going to be a fine day, Antonio. What have you planned?" asked
Francisco.

Antonio glanced across at Don Miguel as he answered, "I was hoping I
could spend some time visiting with Martina—after the work's finished."

Don Miguel looked up quickly. "What do you and the curandera find to
talk so much about, Antonio?"

She teaches me many things about plants. Everytime I see her, I learn
something new. The last time, she went into the process by which a person
can recover oils from different plants. Her method's amazing."

"Do you really want to be a curandero?" Rebecca asked, doubting. "I
can't see you as a healer. I've always pictured you as a handsome vaquero
...roping and riding...dashing across the plains and valleys on Chula."

"My dear little sister! I can do all those things you picture and still help
people in need. To be a curandero sometimes is not one's choice. Our God
above designates some people to serve Him further by serving others. But I
can't really explain the feeling I get when I discover the magical healing of
herbs. And I can't learn enough about them. I want to know more and more
about herbs," Antonio told her.

His mother, ever attentive to her children, served Antonio another
helping. Then she said—more to the entire family—"If Antonio feels this call
and he is willing to accept it with all the responsibilities that accompany it,
then we shall be proud of him. In helping others, we are helping ourselves."

Don Miguel listened to them quietly. He was deeply convinced Antonio
could blend the tasks of a patrón with those of a curandero. He had great
faith in his son's abilities.

Gloria spoke. "Aren't you afraid of the brujos and brujas, Antonio?" She worried about her brother.

"No, my little sister. There is nothing to fear from them if you're in complete control of your mind and body and have a healthy spiritual outlook. I want to visit La Concha, the bruja. I want to learn about the blackmagic she's supposed to excel in. When the time is right—and when I'm more familiar with healing herbs—I want to understand what's called blackmagic," Antonio answered, trying to reassure Gloria.

"I hope you are all ready for Marianela's birthday celebration tomorrow. We must be at Don Crescencio's before sunset. And you must deliver the filly, Antonio. Is she ready?" Don Miguel asked.

"She is, papa," Antonio answered.

"I'm really surprised how well she's turned out," Francisco said, proud of his brother's ability. "You trained her in such a short time!"

"Marianela's going to be so pleased," Gloria added.

"Cara Linda still needs some work...her backing up still isn't the best," Antonio said with a tinge of embarrassment at the flattery.

"And this morning I must butcher those cabritos we're taking. One of the vaqueros can take them to the Salas hacienda this afternoon. Crescencio is expecting them. Now! It is time we start our work," Miguel signaled, pushing back his chair and placing his napkin in its ring.

That afternoon—with his assigned chores of the day behind him—Antonio walked to Martina's small adobe house which sat on a low knoll on the south edge of San Lucas. He noticed a strand of garlic hanging over the door frame as he knocked on the door. He knew the garlic was to keep evil spirits away. In a moment, the door opened. Before him stood a small, waspish woman in her early seventies. Her long, black hair gave the impression of a much younger person—it didn't fit with the deeply lined, wrinkled face. Yet it was her clear, dark eyes that made for intrigue.

"Buenas tardes, Martina," Antonio greeted her. "With your permission, may I visit you awhile?"

"What need do you have today of Martina, my young friend?"

"I hoped we could sit awhile and you could tell me more about herbs."

"The old lady gave a low laugh, revealing her pleasure at being sought out. "Come in! I had the feeling you were coming to visit me. You know I am always willing to share what I know with someone who is sincere in his quest for knowledge. I feel you are, Antonio."

He followed her into the small front room she used for receiving as well as for her workroom. "Each time I visit you, there are more new herbs hanging from the ceiling," he commented.

Martina nodded and smiled. "Sit here beside me, Antonio." She motioned to the buffalo hide in front of the fireplace.

Martina's room was neatly kept and nothing was ever out of place. *It's as if each thing is expecting to be called upon for service at any moment,* Antonio thought as he took his seat.

"And what specifically would you like to discuss?"

"I wanted to ask what you recommend for people when they suffer with Gran Mal—the tremors, shaking and convulsions."

"There are many different plants, when used in a tea or applied to various areas of the body as an ointment which will help to quiet Gran Mal," Martina replied gravely. "Tolache, for example. Some call it jimson weed. Then there are roots of different cacti which I also use." She went into great detail about the preparation of the plants, the time to pick them, the correct way to dry them and preserve them. Antonio was so absorbed in listening and making mental notes he failed to notice it was growing dark. When he realized the hour was late, he exclaimed, "I must excuse myself, Martina. The evening chores!" He didn't mention he needed to work Cara Linda once more before he delivered the horse to Marianela.

"I know. I know. So much work." Martina said. Before he left, she looked deep into his eyes and said, "Let me have your hand! And I want to touch your head, Antonio." As he stood before her, she touched him saying in a muffled voice, "Yes, yes! Horses! You must always be alert around horses. I feel...somehow a horse may change your life, my son."

"What do you mean, Martina? For good or worse?"

"I can't say. I don't know. But you must be very cautious when you are working with horses," she replied with a far away look in her eyes.

"But I'm around horses every day."

"Even so...promise me you will be very careful!"

"And if I am not?" he asked.

Martina closed her eyes and shuddered. Then she went into the house and left him standing alone in the doorway.

Walking home, Antonio wondered, *What was it she saw? Probably just her motherly instinct...horses, indeed.* In a strange way, he felt offended by her premonition, or whatever it was...

When he arrived home, Chula and her colt were loose in the courtyard. "What're you doing here, Chula? How'd you get out of your stall?"

Francisco came running. "Chula's acting strange. She's knocked down the logs you placed at the entrance of her stall, then she ran in here. Someone left the puertón open."

"Why would she want to come into the courtyard?" Antonio asked.

"Maybe she's in heat."

"Not yet."

"Maybe she's looking for you."

"Why didn't you put her back in her stall?"

"She wouldn't let me near her. I've never seen her like this."

Antonio took the horse's halter and patted her on the shoulder. "What's the matter, girl? What's going on with you?"

The animal responded to his soothing words with a low whinny.

"I think you're right, Francisco. She wants to find a stallion. I'll take her to the corral and fix the gate. Thanks for looking after her."

For the second time Antonio thought of Martina's warning: was the frightened horse an omen—or merely a coincidence?

Next morning Marianela's brothers, Alfonso and Bernardo, joined their father outside Marianela's window to serenade her on her birthday. Bernardo played the guitar as they sang the haunting *Las Mañanitas*, sung to start the day of the birthday celebrant. Marianela listened to them from her window. When they finished, she went down into the garden and embraced them.

"Thank you! Oh, thank you! It was lovely!" she exclaimed.

The others in the family joined Marianela and the troubadors and happily gave their birthday greetings.

"You are as beautiful today on your twentieth birthday as you were on your first, Marianela!" Don Crescencio teased his daughter. "But now my wish for you is that in the next twenty years you will develop into as fine a woman as your mother." He put his arm around his wife.

"The day's gone so fast!" Marianela fretted as she and her sisters dressed that evening for the party. "The guests will be here soon and I can hear the musicians tuning their instruments—I haven't finished my hair!"

The Salas hacienda was festive, ready to receive. There were mountains of food, topped by the barbequed cabritos and stuffed, roast piglet, not to

mention cabrito blood cooked with garlic, onions and piñon nuts, bur-
roniates (the coiled lengths of entrails, stuffed with fat and spices) cooked
slowly over the coals, and bowls of chili, squash with corn, beans and the
heaps of fresh breads and tortillas. There were kegs of fine wine and milder
drinks for children and non-drinkers.

Candles burned softly against dark adobe walls and lanterns created a
romantic setting for this birthday party Marianela would remember and
cherish.

The guests began to arrive. Most brought gifts or remembrances of some
kind. When Don Crescencio was told Don Miguel had entered the courtyard with his family, he rushed to meet them. He was not only eager to greet
his friend and his family but to saddle Cara Linda with the special saddle
and bridle he had had made.

"Miguel! Rosamaria! My friends, welcome!" he called as they entered.
Antonio was riding Chula, proudly leading Cara Linda.

"Is Marianela inside?" Antonio asked.

"Yes, We must hurry and saddle her horse before she comes out," her
father answered.

"That's a very fine saddle!" Francisco exclaimed.

"As well as the bridle," Antonio added.

"What gifts! You'll spoil the girl, Crescencio," Dona Rosamaria said.

Don Crescencio answered with a broad smile and sent Bernardo into
the house. "Ask your mother and sisters to come into the
courtyard...especially Marianela."

Ofelia had already told Marianela, "Antonio's here with his family!" so
she rushed out before the others to greet Don Miguel's family. In her amaze-
ment, seeing Antonio leading Cara Linda, she almost forgot her manners.
"How did you get Cara Linda? What are you doing with her, Antonio?"

Before Antonio could reply, Don Crescencio motioned everyone to
gather around him and Marianela. "My beautiful and fine daughter! My
birthday present for you is ready," he said, pointing to Cara Linda. "Now
our secret is out. Antonio has been training Cara Linda for you. If what I
hear is correct, he has trained her with his usual competency. The saddle
and bridle are little extras. Cara Linda must look her best for you when you
are riding. Happy birthday, my princess! I hope you are pleased."

The overwhelmed girl threw her arms around her father and kissed him.
"Papa! What can I say? I can't tell you how happy I am. You couldn't have

pleased me more. I have the most wonderful father in the world. Thank you!" Tears came to her eyes. She wiped them with a lace handkerchief, her sister's gift. "And now Cara Linda is trained. You've made me happier knowing you had the best trainer for her," Marianela said bestowing a smile on Antonio. "Now when I ride her and use the handsome saddle, I'll always remember you and the secret you kept so well. Please come in everyone and help me celebrate my birthday. I am honored by your presence."

As the gathering filed into the hacienda, Marianela took Antonio's arm. "You must tell me all you've taught Cara Linda. She looks so different. Oh, Antonio! How I've dreamed of the day I could ride her. Now you've made it possible. Just look how she stands...so confident."

"I've taught her all I could in such a short time," he replied. "She does learn quickly. And I was surprised how gentle she was when she took the first saddle. She's a fine horse. Ride her as often as you can."

"I will."

"She has some special little mannerisms...you'll pick up on them. When we have more time, I'll tell you the ways she responds to different situations." As he talked, Antonio's thoughts were about the girl who stood so near him. *She's radiant...the loveliest girl in the whole world*, he thought as he said, "And I'm deeply honored to have participated in this gift."

As a servant took Cara Linda to her stall, Antonio held Marianela's hand and they walked toward the covered outdoor patio where dancing couples moved to the lively music.

"You are very beautiful tonight, Marianela," Antonio whispered. "More beautiful than ever! I like your dress. I always think of you in white. Your hair shines so...it challenges the night."

Marianela blushed with the compliments. Her heart pounded as she replied, laughing gaily, "And you are so handsome in your leather jacket and pants. I've never seen so many silver buttons on a man's suit. Did you sew them?"

"A Mexican tailor in Santa Fe made the suit for me and mother had all these buttons. One day she and my sisters sewed them on the suit. I asked how they expected me to dance with you, for if I slip I'll never get up with all this weight. And now, may I have this dance? I promise not to fall." Laughing together, they joined the other dancers.

Antonio never left Marianela's side as other guests continued to arrive and offer her congratulations. When she spoke with others, his eyes were only on her. When they were dancing, Marianela remarked, "This is the first time we've danced together since we were young children. Do you remember that fiesta at your hacienda when you stepped on my dress and I cried?"

"I did? I'm very sorry. I hope I apologized."

"Silly thing to remember, isn't it? I'm sure you said you didn't mean to."

Through the small talk while they danced, Antonio was never happier. "You're like holding a feather...the music is great...will you teach me to dance?"

"You dance very well. I don't need to teach you," Marianela replied, looking up into his eyes thinking *His arms are strong...his hand gentle. I have such a peculiar feeling, being close to him...*

When the music stopped, Don Crescencio approached them. "Everyone's eyes were on you during that dance, my children. It was a pleasure watching you. Now, if you'll forgive your father, I'd like a word with your partner. I have some business to discuss with him."

"I don't know if I should trust you two...you with your secrets! Perhaps for a minute?" Marianela answered.

As her father led Antonio aside, Faustín Pino came up to Marianela and asked for the next dance, then whisked her away to the music. Antonio's attention was more on Marianela, not what Crescencio had to say. *Faustín is a good friend...no need to worry, I suppose...* he thought as Don Crescencio said, "If you can spare not looking at my daughter a moment, Antonio, I would like to thank you again for training the horse and I want to pay you. What is your usual fee?"

"You owe me nothing, Don Crescencio. I won't hear of pay. Your daughter's happiness means everything to me," Antonio heard himself say. Later that night when he was alone in his room, he trembled remembering his sudden braveness. "Her smile is my reward. But there is something I will ask of you. I would like permission to call at your hacienda and visit with Marianela. I ask you as a gentleman and with assurance I will treat Marianela with the greatest respect."

An overwhelming feeling of loneliness came over Don Crescencio at that instant. He thought, *the inevitable...I will lose my daughter*, as he gravely replied, "You have my permission. I can expect no other behavior than that of a gentleman, which I know you are. As you know, I have the highest respect for your family and you. I will inform Dona Thomasita of your request. We will expect you to call on Marianela...and welcome you."

Antonio bowed as the two shook hands; as he returned to the dancing, he felt ten feet tall. *I want to shout...yell...announce to all "I'm going to call on Marianela!"* But there was the girl he adored in the arms of Faustín!

On his way to cut in, Antonio bumped into his sister, Gloria. "You almost knocked me over, Antonio!" she exaggerated. "What's the hurry?" All the time knowing why he was rushing.

"I beg your pardon!" And whispering in her ear, she was the first to hear his news, "Don Crescencio's given me permission to call on Marianela!"

In four steps he was at Faustín's shoulder.

"May I cut in?" What could his friend do but politely acquiesce? Once again Marianela was in his arms.

Delighted he'd returned, she pretended to be piqued. "Why didn't you let Faustín finish the dance? Why are you acting like a...wild man? What's wrong with you?" she scolded.

"I suppose I was a bit abrupt. I couldn't wait to tell you...your father's given me permission to call on you!"

The couple whirled about the floor looking into each other's eyes, both somewhat stunned by this sudden turn. Finally Marianela laughed, "But you didn't ask me if you could ask him."

"I surprised myself. I didn't intend...Oh, yes!...I did intend to ask him but I hadn't thought when I'd ask. I just blurted it out," Antonio confessed.

"You do want me to call on you, don't you?"

"Oh, yes! I want you to..." she replied, still smiling at him as she thought "He's so serious. So good-looking when he has that little worry frown."

Relieved of that unnecessary concern, Antonio's spirits soared. He felt like he was floating. At the same time, he tugged at his collar, flushed with excitement. "Please, Marianela! I feel so warm. Let's walk out in the court-yard. I need some cool air," he pleaded. She took his arm and they went into the main courtyard where the lights from the house flickered and winked. Alone with her, a lump came into his throat again.

There's so much to tell her, to say. How can I start? I want to tell her every-thing I feel, he thought as he said, "The stars are all out tonight. They want to be here for your birthday...to see you..."

"I like that. It's a pretty thought."

"I would give them all to you. I'd give you the universe, Marianela. I am yours, if you will have me, he added softly. When she raised her face to his, he saw his answer, her acceptance of his gift.

There was an ancient cottonwood tree near the wooden well house in the center of the courtyard and underneath the tree were built small bancos where they sat, his arm about her waist, her head against his shoulder.

"I can't seem to catch my breath," she sighed. "So fast! Yet, I longed for this moment. Now that it's here...Oh, Antonio! I don't hesitate to give you my answer. Yes! Yes! Yes! I want you to be mine. I care for you. What I feel for you grows each time I see you. I think about you each day."

"I love you, Marianela," he murmured. "I've rehearsed over and over what I would tell you when I asked you to be mine, but now all that matters is, I love you."

"And I love you."

Antonio reached out and cupped her face in his hands. "What an exquisite face and that boquita de oro! I must feel its warmth, he exclaimed. His lips pressed hers and they each found a part of the other becoming one.

"Someone will see us," Marianela said breathlessly, but she again yielded to his kiss. What seemed a moment became an eternity within their hearts. Marianela touched Antonio's lips. "Antonio, please! You have given me a moment I shall never forget. Now give me a moment to tell you how many times I've wanted you to kiss me."

"I don't know if this happens to everyone in love," Antonio said, "but since the last time we were together, I've had an incessant longing for you. You are everywhere with me—when I ride or when I'm working, you are there. I miss seeing you. I couldn't wait any longer to ask your father's permission to call on you. The days were already beginning to feel like years. I love you so very much."

"I've also felt all these things, Antonio. I do love you," Marianela said again, his arms tightening around her waist as he pulled her close.

A sudden voice broke their spell.

"Ole! Ole! What is this magical night doing to you young people?" It was Don Miguel. He'd stepped out into the courtyard for a breath of air.

"Oh, papa! We were on our way back to the dance," Antonio fumbled.

"Don Miguel, you've not honored me with a dance yet," Marianela said swiftly coming to his rescue.

"Perhaps we three should return to the dance?" Don Miguel said lightly as Marianela took his hand. They went in, the music swelled and Don Miguel led Marianela to the floor. Antonio made his way to the wine cask where Francisco found him.

"Where did you go? You missed the solo guitar and Rebecca's song. No one could find Marianela," Francisco said in a mock-mysterious voice.

"Oh, yes, we did step out for a minute."

"I don't blame you," Francisco said.

"Don Crescencio's given me permission to call on her, Francisco."

Francisco's enthusiasm was genuine—so was his prying curiosity: "Did you kiss her?" he asked.

"Go find a dancing partner, little brother!"

When Francisco left, it struck Antonio he'd forgotten to give Marianela the poem he'd written for her. *She must think I didn't bring her a gift. I should have remembered when we were under the stars.*

He went in to find her but every male guest seemed to be claiming a dance. *I mustn't feel jealous. Who can resist her?* he asked himself.

After politely waiting his turn, she was once again in his arms and he said: "Outside I felt the warmth only you make me feel! It almost made me forget—I brought you a gift. If we could only go out to the portal...that is...if you will stop dancing with all these men..."

Under a lantern, he took the poem from his pocket and offered it to her. "I hope you like it. Happy birthday, Marianela!"

Her lips moved softly to his words as she read to herself: "...Everything belongs to her. White is her color..."

Finishing, she looked up at him.

His heart sank; he thought, *it doesn't please her.*

Then Marianela said, "You are so sensitive. Your words touch me in a way I can't describe. I love your poem. I love you!"

And drawing him near, she kissed him. "There! I don't care who sees us. I don't care who knows what I feel: I want everyone to know."

Antonio was enthralled and speechless.

Antonio and his family didn't feel like starting another day of work next morning. Eventually, after discussing events of the previous evening, they heard from Antonio. He told of his intentions.

"I am happy for you, my son, as all of us are. Marianela is the kind of woman who will be a fine wife. I advise you to go slowly so that you two can develop a strong relationship. Be certain you know each other well," Don Miguel approved. "Remember, marriage is not to be entered into lightly."

As the weeks went by, Antonio called on Marianela faithfully, either in the evenings or when he rode by her house on the way to his family's rancho. At times he was granted permission to ride with her in the countryside to search for herbs—always with Rafaela or Ofelia keeping a watchful eye. Even so, there were moments for stolen kisses.

The colorful fall was coming to an end. One day while the young couple walked in the garden, now bravely holding hands in view of all, Marianela said, "These days are so golden. I wish they'd never end. I love the warmth of the October sun, the odor of the ripening pears. But soon, we'll feel the winter's cold. Will we be able to be together as often then, Antonio?"

More deeply in love than ever, he sighed. "I hope more. It's time for me to talk with my parents, Marianela. Don't you agree?"

"I do. Oh, yes, I agree!"

That evening as Antonio sat in front of the fireplace with his family after dinner, he gathered his courage. "Mama. Papa. I have something to ask of you, if you'll be so kind as to hear my request."

"Tell us what it is, my son," Don Miguel replied.

"I would like for you to request Marianela's hand in marriage for me. Will you speak to her parents? She and I have discussed this many times and we feel we are ready to become man and wife. We love each other dearly."

Don Miguel listened attentively and when Antonio finished, took off his spectacles and put the periodical he'd been reading on the table. Don Miguel ceremoniously lit his cigar and, putting one arm behind him before he spoke, he paced several times in front of the fire. He cleared his throat as if he intended to give a long speech, but instead broke out with a broad smile and said, "We are happy for you. Your mother and I have also discussed your relationship. We only wondered when you would make this request. We will be proud to ask for Marianela's hand in marriage. We want you to know that your choice is our choice." He then extended his hand to congratulate Antonio and embraced him.

Dona Rosamaria beckoned Antonio and kissed him. "Both your father and I have prayed you and Marianela would wed." She added knowingly, "I don't expect a refusal from Don Crescencio and Dona Thomasita."

Francisco clapped Antonio on the shoulder. "I certainly approve," he exclaimed with a swagger.

Rebecca and Gloria couldn't contain their excitement. "Just think! How proud I'll feel to have her as a sister," Gloria told Antonio with a hug.

"Marianela will certainly be a welcome addition to this family. Who knows, someday I may marry Ofelia," Francisco went on in his bragging manner.

"I will set a date with Don Crescencio and your mother and I will call on him and his wife. Now, to bed! There is much work in the morning." With that, Don Miguel dismissed the family. As Dona Rosamaria extinguished the lamps, she took his hand. "I'm very happy he made the decision." "So am I," Don Miguel answered and the two went into their room.

Marianela sought an opportune time to talk with her mother about the marriage plans. She always talked first with Dona Thomasita about intimate matters, relying on her mother, in turn, to discuss the problem or situation with Don Crescencio in private. That was the custom. So one morning—the air was brisk with a light, cold wind blowing out of the north and the fragrant odor of fresh-baked bread permeated Dona Thomasita's kitchen—Marianela helped her mother with the breakfast. Dona Thomasita usually fed at least a dozen workers besides her own family each morning and relied on her daughter's help. As it was round-up time, there were extra cattle hands to feed. The kitchen was a scene of bustle, feeding the starving men. Emma contributed more than her share to the commotion. Ever at Dona Thomasita's side, the clatter she made with the dishes sounded intentional. Never to miss anything, she'd stop when there was conversation to listen to, then resume her noise-making during silences. Emma also kept a sharp eye on the daughters of the household, consequently Marianela had a difficult time catching her mother's attention without Emma knowing. But in the zaguán she managed to whisper, "Mama, I would like to discuss something—away from Emma's ears."

"The dishes are finished. We'll go to your bedroom to talk," her mother answered. "But we can't talk long. I must start preparing dinner. I'll be glad when the round-up is over!" They passed along the outside portal and entered Marianela's bedroom. Dona Thomasita settled comfortably on the foot of her daughter's bed. "I think I know what is on your mind, dear. But go ahead—tell me your problem," the knowing mother said with a smile.

Marianela blushed. "You are always wise, mama."

"I take pride in knowing my children."

"Then it's no surprise. You know Antonio and I want to be married.

He'll be asking his parents to make their formal call to ask for me in marriage. I wanted you to know before they call."

"So much secrecy! Well, your father and I have been waiting for the day. And you know I am happy for you, if this is your decision. I'm sure your father's feelings are the same as mine." Dona Thomasita rose and put her arms about her daughter. "I hope you will be happy, Marianela. I know you will. Antonio is an intelligent young man. I will love him like a son." Looking into Marianela's beaming face she sighed. "The first marriage in our family. Well, there is much to discuss, so many plans...preparations for a wedding. When do you wish to set the date?"

"We hope to be married the first week of May next year. It's only mid-November. Won't that give us enough time, mama?"

"Of course, that's plenty of time...six months."

"Antonio says May is the month of new life. He wants us to start ours then. And his birthday is in May," Marianela chattered happily to her mother as they returned to the kitchen and Emma's raised eyebrows.

Antonio reserved moments of each busy workday to spend with his herbs. His reputation was developing now as a knowledgeable person and many began to consult him in the treatment of their illnesses. He would always say, however, "I know so little...there is so much to learn." One day, a man who believed himself a victim of witchcraft sought Antonio's advice. "I know nothing about herbs used to remove illnesses caused by witchcraft," Antonio told him honestly, "I must visit La Concha. Everyone says she is a bruja but perhaps she will teach me what I need to know."

One chilly evening in November, Antonio paid a call on the witch. On the way to her house, he recalled what he'd heard: she doesn't care for visitors and she doesn't appreciate people asking questions. But on he went to the small hut at the edge of the river on the outskirts of San Lucas.

Her house was perched precariously on a clay bank. It was barely visible because the chaparral and cottonwood trees hugged it closely. Except for the flocks of ravens which nested in the trees, it looked quite deserted.

Antonio approached and the big, startled blackbirds flapped in every direction, rawkishly calling attention to his visit. The beating of their clapping wings was almost deafening and would have frightened a timid caller.

Antonio remembered Martina's words: "Be very careful. La Concha has the ability to change into many forms—animal and inanimate. I suspect she can do the same to anyone she doesn't like." He asked himself, *Should I have come to see her? Am I visiting this woman because I want to know about healing illnesses or is it her mystical powers that fascinate me?* A raven flew in front of him and jarred him back to reality. He stood before a small, wooden door with huge cracks and rusty hinges.

He pulled the iron door clanger. Soon the door swung open. The hinges creaked. Before him stood an old woman with pure, white hair, dressed in a long, black gown which came to her ankles. Antonio's first thoughts as she opened the door were, *Her face is like a valentine. Even though she's bent with age, she's very tall. Is she Indian?*

"I have been waiting your visit," La Concha said. Her voice reminded him of the wind rustling over dried weeds in winter. "Come in Antonio! I hope my friends the ravens did not frighten you."

"I must admit my thoughts were miles away when I arrived and they did give me a start but I wasn't really frightened. I like...all birds," he replied. Then he added politely, "I hope it is an opportune time to visit. I've been wanting to call on you for some time, Concha."

"It is a fine time for you to visit," she nodded. "Don't stand on such ceremony. Please! I offer you the hospitality of my humble abode." She motioned for him to sit on a small banco next to the fireplace where a low fire burned. "You are known to be kind and generous, so please excuse the clutter," she said with a wave of her hand, dismissing the untidy room. "I am not on this earth to be a good housekeeper. I wish my mission in life were that easy. Instead, as you know, I'm dedicated to helping those who feel they have no heavenly answers for their woes. To the point, I work in the art of witchcraft. But then you already know that." And she laughed. "That must not frighten you or you would not visit me."

At that moment, Antonio glanced at a pair of owl wings tacked on the wall; there were those who were afraid of the owl but Antonio knew the bird as a symbol of wisdom.

"Concha, I respect your powers. I think you have much to give, wisdom especially. I hope my wisdom will increase and that through it, I will be able to help people some day."

"Now, let us come to the point. What do you wish to know, Antonio?"

"First, tell me—do you place a curse on anyone you are requested to curse? Or do you select those whom you feel deserve a curse.?"

"Ah, that!" she sighed and for the first time she seemed to relax her aged frame. "I will tell you. Many people come to me and ask me to do harm to those who have harmed them. Others come to test me, to see if I really know my art. They ask peculiar questions. And there are others who wish me to bestow a curse—a call for the wish of death—on another. I'm asked to do many things. It is difficult to decide how I will use my magic. But I would say my decisions hinge on what I sense and feel about the person making the request. If I feel the person only wants revenge and is too lazy or inept to undertake it himself, then I refuse. On the other hand, if someone calls on me to place him on an equal footing with an adversary, I'm usually more receptive. You understand, once a curse is initiated by me, there is no going back. It would take a miracle to undo the power of my work."

As she spoke, Antonio felt strength emanate from the old woman. Then she finished speaking and a large bull snake slithered across his feet and slid out a crack in the door. Antonio tried to restrain his surprise for Concha's gaze was still intent upon him, and either she didn't see the snake or she ignored it. With a slight tremble in his voice, he replied, "I understand what you're saying: you don't cast your spells simply because you have the power. But I'm sure you can also remove an evil ojo from a person."

"I can."

"What I seek from you is the knowledge I might use to release people from these mystical spells," he told her.

Concha's laugh was cynical. "For such a young man, you ask a lot."

"You may think I want to undo your spells, Concha, but I am primarily interested in helping those whom the curse would destroy."

"That is the reason for the curse!" she snapped.

Antonio sighed. "I didn't think you would impart the knowledge I ask. But as you know, other brujos besides you are also casting evil spells. I must continue to seek answers to my requests either from you or them."

"You do not waste words," Concha said contemptuously.

"Maybe I should not have been so forthright."

"You are young and lack experience. And you are foolishly naive to believe I would share the secrets that could enable you to dispell my work."

"I was afraid you wouldn't..."

"You must seek and search. You have much to learn. Perhaps someday when the time is right I will feel more disposed to teach you what I know."

The old woman lapsed into pensive silence, staring into space. Antonio fidgeted, wondering if she were through with him. But after some moments she looked over at him and said, "One thing more I will say to you. Do not ever ask for a confrontation with me. I like the man I see in you and it would disturb me very much to hurt you. If you work against me, do your healing around the edges of my spells...otherwise..."

He didn't ask her to finish her sentence and instead he asked, "There is something else you could tell me, Concha. Who is this man they call Juanito the brujo, who lives high in the Ortiz mountains south of us?"

Her thin lips twisted in a wry line and she chuckled like an old hen. "Juanito! Sometimes an ally; other times my worst adversary. You should visit him in your quest."

"Is he as close to the earth as people say? I've heard Juanito converses with all of God's creations."

"I respect him. Now, I have said all I will say about Juanito." Concha stood—Antonio could hear the creaking of her bones as she rose—indicating in her way the interview was over.

"With your permission, Concha, I will take my leave. Thank you for allowing me to speak with you today."

Antonio went toward the door but before he opened it, she asked, "How are you and Marianela getting along these days?"

Her question caught him off guard. "Why...fine, thank you!" he said.

He saw Concha close her eyes and open them and she stared at the ceiling in a trance. She murmured sleepily: "A horse...a horse...it isn't clear." Then looking at Antonio, she cautioned in low tones as if she were afraid of being overheard, "Careful! You...and the girl must be careful!"

As he left she called, "I wish you both the best of good fortune. Return, Antonio, whenever you need me. If I am not here, my ravens will tell you where to find me."

Antonio shivered hearing the crone's laugh as he went out into the cold night. A nagging fear came over him as he walked the path from her house. *A horse...again! What is this? Why should Concha and Martina both warn me about horses? They know something. But how can I stay away from horses? They're part of my life...as well as Marianela's This is all so strange. Both of those old women are strange. But I suppose people will say that I am one day—if not already. One day I must make the journey to Juanito—wherever he may be.*

The day arrived when Antonio's parents were to make the prendorio, or engagement call on Marianela's parents. As intimate as the two families were, they kept strict rules when it came to customs; the engagement call was formal. The evening Don Miguel and Dona Rosamaria arrived at Don Crescencio's hacienda, the wind blew hard from the northeast. There were flurries of snow, yet the wind's biting chill was forgotten in the heart-warming nature of their mission.

Don Crescencio was in the courtyard ready to greet them as they dismounted from their carriage and ushered them into the sala de recibo. A great fire crackled in the adobe fireplace.

"Welcome, dear friends!" Dona Thomasita exclaimed as they entered. Cups of warm mestela awaited them. Thomasita led Rosamaria aside to chat.

As he drank the wild parsley and whiskey tea, Miguel said, "This will warm our bones. Thank you!"

"I fear we are in for a severe winter. Only this morning I pointed out to my sons that all the fur-bearing creatures have thicker coats this year. Tonight may be a preview of what is in store for us, Miguel," Crescencio said.

"Yes, we have noticed the thick matting of hair on the horses and cows. But let the moisture come! I don't have to tell you we need, it, Crescencio."

"Let's hope we have enough firewood for the winter." Seeing the women stare at them in expectation of getting on with the business at hand, Crescencio indicated to Miguel they were ready to listen to him.

Miguel took a final sip of tea and began. "With your permission, good friends, my wife and I have come to ask for Marianela's hand in marriage to our son, Antonio. At this time, I would like to read our written request. We hope you will be able to give us your answer tonight, if possible."

The written request was romantic and flowery, describing the beauty and attributes of the girl. The words were tender and meant as a poetic document which would not only endear the young man but also remain as a testament of his love and faith.

According to custom, when the parents of the girl received these requests, they would in turn give their answer in writing. If they rejected the suitor, it was called a "calabaza"—referring to the lowly squash. If the answer were affirmative, a prendorio had been accomplished and the two young people were betrothed.

Although Antonio's and Marianela's parents were aware of each other's thoughts and feelings about the engagement, they maintained strict adherence to the old customs and the formalities of their ancestors.

Don Crescencio bowed to his guests after Miguel finished. "Don Miguel and Dona Rosamaria, our answer to your request is a very simple, joyous yes! Our written acceptance will verify our word. Now, a toast! For we will soon be compadres. Let us drink to our children who will soon be wed." As he raised his glass, everyone followed suit and the room was full of smiles.

"To love!" Don Crescencio saluted.

"To love!" the others said. "To love!"

"I always feel love permeating this room," Dona Rosamaria said. "But tonight, more than ever."

"Thank you, my dear," Dona Thomasita replied. "Well, it's done! I'm certain our children were ready for this months ago."

"But both are respectful. They are mindful of a time to wait..."

"Neither would consider to act without knowing of our feelings," Don Crescencio added with an approving nod.

"We will be proud to become your compadres," Don Miguel told Don Crescencio clapping him on the shoulder.

"As will we," Dona Thomasita smiled warmly at Antonio's parents. "And now the hour is getting late. Our mission is accomplished, Miguel. Our children will be anxiously waiting to hear what has transpired. We must return home."

"Antonio will worry we're bringing him a squash!" Don Miguel laughed. "And he'll probably ride out to meet us if we stay any longer with you—however pleasant your company and fireside."

"Marianela won't be able to sleep until she has heard," her mother said. "Now, the preparations!" Dona Thomasita sighed.

"I don't envy you," Dona Rosamaria empathized.

"Your turn will come!" The two women laughed gaily, knowing this would be only the first of many weddings in their families. Custom dictated the bride's family bear the expense of the wedding. "Wait until your girls are ready to marry!" Don Thomasita declared in jest.

"Crescencio, please call on me for anything we can provide—for the church, reception or dance. Anything, my friend," Don Miguel said.

Don Crescencio graciously accepted his offer but each knew the proud family would never ask Antonio's family to help defray the cost.

"Come now, Rosamaria, we must start home," Miguel reminded his wife and the two went out into the snowy night.

When the carriage rolled into the courtyard, Antonio's parents saw him standing in the kitchen, holding a lantern and peering through the window.

"He's waiting for us." Rosamaria smiled.

"What did you expect? That he'd be asleep?"

"Poor boy!"

"I wish I had a squash..."

"You wouldn't!"

"Just to tease him."

Antonio raced out to meet them. "What did they say? Yes or no?"

"Don Crescencio sent you something...looks like an overripe calabaza to me," Don Miguel said with a perfectly straight face.

But the mother wouldn't allow her son to suffer. "Antonio, it's not true. Their answer is yes. They are delighted to have you as a son-in-law."

Let's get out of this cold wind," Don Miguel said, "and we will tell you each detail of our conversation." Then both parents embraced their son.

Marianela, only one room away, saw the look on her parents' faces and knew the answer she longed for. She flew into her father's arms crying in joy. "Oh, mama! Papa! Thank you so much! You know I love Antonio... we're so much in love. And I love you for knowing our love is true and for allowing us to wed. You've made me the happiest girl in the world."

"What we did was only done for love," Don Crescencio returned, his eyes brimming with tears.

"May we start setting the dates, mother?" Marianela asked eagerly.

"Now?" Dona Thomasita asked in surprise. "No. Your father is tired and so am I. We'll talk in the morning."

"I'll never sleep tonight," she wailed.

"You don't want Antonio to see you with circles under your eyes, do you?" her father chided. "Now, to bed. There's time enough tomorrow for you and your mother to start planning."

"Don't forget the other girls. They'll not be left out of this." Dona Thomasita kissed Marianela and reminded, "Please don't wake them if they're asleep, Marianela."

"They'll be angry if I wait till tomorrow to tell them."

"Let them be angry then," her father said smiling proudly. "To bed...to sleep, my soon-to-be-married daughter!"

Before entering her room, Marianela called to her parents just as they were closing their door. "Will it cost much, papa? I mean, the wedding..."

"Don't you worry. Leave that to me, Marianela," he assured her.

"Didn't you know your papa is rich?" his wife quipped to which Don Crescencio laughingly replied, "Before the wedding!"

When the first heavy snows blanketed the countryside around San Lucas, the herders and vaqueros enclosed their sheep and cattle in winter pastures and throughout the winter the men rode sturdy horses through deep snow in careful vigilance feeding the stock that could no longer browse and forage for food. Cattle and sheep were often put on southern and western slopes of the mountains where the snow melted faster. Don Miguel and Don Crescencio never underestimated winter and helped each other— as well as their neighbors—tending the cattle and sheep which numbered into the thousands. The winters were long. No one traveled at night except in an emergency and then with extreme caution.

With the advent of winter, Antonio started to fret. His weekly visit to Marianela was, of necessity, made only in daytime and because the daylight hours were needed for work, his visit grew shorter and shorter. In the evenings as he sat with his family, he was always restless.

"Why do you pace so, Antonio? Can't you sit still?" Francisco said.

"I'll be happy when Spring arrives, won't you, mother?" Don Miguel said. "Then Antonio will spare your carpet. Maybe we can repair the path he's made this winter."

Antonio excused himself. "I'm going to my room, if I may?"

"To study herbs or write poems to Marianela?" Francisco needled.

"You may be excused. Goodnight, Antonio." Don Miguel said, but when he was out of earshot, he reprimanded his younger son. "You may be stricken with the same disease some day, Francisco."

"I hope so!" his wife interrupted.

"So you shouldn't tease him," Don Miguel continued.

"I'm not going to act like him...jumping about like a flea." Francisco shot back.

"And you are excused, also, Francisco!" Don Miguel commanded.

"But, papa! It's early..."

"You heard me!"

"Goodnight mama. Papa." And off he went to his room.

The winter was the longest Antonio had ever spent. "Will the snow ever melt?" he wondered. One early February day he watched the soft flakes fall and his heart sank. "Another storm!" The incurable romantic within was already writing a poem, thinking he'd give it to her at the first sign of spring:

> *We will walk hand in hand*
> *Over the meadows of Life,*
> *Seeking to make our love grow*
> *with each passing day.*
>
> *Together we shall share all God's creations,*
> *And loving care give to them,*
> *As He has given us one-to-another.*
>
> *When our work is done here on earth,*
> *Lovers everywhere will sing our song.*
> *An endless melody and tune,*
> *With words that speak of love*
> *which has no end.*

Antonio mused, *Our love will truly be endless. May the brilliant stars in the heavens be my judge, I will make her a good husband.*

And it was the same for Marianela; up at dawn, bustling with energy, preparing for her wedding. Her mother laughed one morning, "This isn't my girl—the one who used to complain of being bored."

"She wakes me so early," Ofelia complained. "Why can't she let me sleep a little later, mama?"

"Marianela has her mind on something special," Dona Thomasita said, plaiting Ofelia's long, dark tresses. "Besides, take heed! Your time will come. Then you'll know what your sister is going through."

"Oh mama! Won't spring ever arrive? Is there no way to help it along?" Marianela chimed playfully, making a long face and turning down the corners of her mouth to demonstrate her suffering. "How I long for the day when Antonio and I will be together each minute! We'll go for the long walks he loves so—looking for herbs, and..."

"You'll be busy cooking, washing dishes, darning his socks!" scoffed Ofelia. "Herbs, indeed!"

"Oh, poof!" Marianela replied with a toss of her head. "What do you know about married life?"

"Girls!" their mother admonished with a smile, patting Ofelia's head—a signal she'd finished the daily task of grooming her hair. "Now, Marianela, today I want you to try on your wedding dress."

That delighted the sisters who were wide-eyed with anticipation as Dona Thomasita went to her leather trunk and opened the repository where she kept such treasures. No one, not even her husband, was allowed to open the special trunk; Dona Thomasita kept the key with her at all times and—needless to say—the trunk was always locked. She lifted the lid and revealed a row of carefully wrapped packages all bound up in pretty ribbon.

"What's in those packages, mama?" Ofelia asked.

"Silks, my dear. For the bride," Dona Thomasita said.

"Can't we see them? Please?"

"By and by, dear. But now, stand aside while I place this on the bed."

The girls could see other neatly done-up packages in the trunk and as their mother took them out one by one and carried them to her bed, they were breathless with excitement.

Finally she came to the last package; this she took to her rocking chair, the one upholstered in horsehair, and she sat down and placed it on her lap.

"Is that the dress?"

"It is," Dona Thomasita said proudly, holding it up for them to see while she carefully shook out the folds.

"Oh, mama!" Marianela gasped.

Ofelia, without thinking, reached out to touch it.

"Don't touch!" her mother warned.

"But, why, mama?"

'Little hands that haven't been washed can leave smudges, my dear. You see, this dress is very fine..."

"It's grand, mother," Marianela exclaimed.

"And I've kept it that way for you girls, as you must keep it for your daughters some day," Dona Thomasita said.

"I don't see why I can't touch it," Ofelia complained. "Besides, I'll never get to wear it. Marianela always gets everything."

"You will in your turn," her mother assured her.

"Did you really wear it when you married papa?"

"I did—twenty-two years ago, believe it or not," she chuckled, patting her waist. "I was much thinner then. And my mother wore it at her wedding," she added fondly.

"Who made it?" Marianela asked.

"It was made by a very famous seamstress in Mexico City who came from France, I believe. She knew all the latest court fashions my mother told me."

"Why Mexico," Ofelia asked.

"That's where my grandparents lived when my mother was a girl, before they came to this land. I've told you that before," Dona Thomasita replied.

"The silk looks just like new, doesn't it?"

"It's very fine silk, Marianela. It was spun in France."

"I love the off-the-shoulder effect! And the lace!"

"The lace was made in Brussels, I believe."

"But the pearls! There must be thousands of them. Look how each is set in the center of the lace! The lace makes petals around them, they look like tiny flowers!" Marianela's face was flushed with excitement as she examined the gown hungrily with her eyes.

"Now! I want you to see this," Dona Thomasita said in a secretive whisper. Then she placed the dress on the bed and began unwrapping another, larger package. Her daughters could hardly believe what they saw: a veil and train that appeared to be made of gossamer.

"How could anyone make lace like that? It's so fine, mother!" Marianela gasped. "And there's silk backing!"

"It is so long!" Ofelia exclaimed. "Your mother must have been a princess."

"Her papa was very wealthy. A man of some renown and prestige."

"I love you for keeping these for us, mama," Marianela said as she hugged her mother and kissed her on the cheek. "I know now why you won't let anyone in this trunk. Oh, thank you, thank you, mama!"

"Remember, some day you girls will have to protect our... treasures." Dona Thomasita reminded them.

"I will, mama," Marianela replied quickly as Ofelia gave them all the benefit of her best pout.

"So, today, let's do some measuring before we take out or let in. Fortunately, the seamstress made this gown so alterations could be made without showing," Dona Thomasita said, taking out her measuring tape.

"What are Rafaela and I going to wear at Marianela's wedding," Ofelia asked, her little jealousy blowing up like a balloon.

"Your dresses will be made by Señora Diaz in Santa Fe."

Ofelia gave a quick smile of approval as she shrugged a shoulder at her older sister. "I like her dresses. They're the *best*! But we don't have to wear white, do we?"

"All you girls will be dressed in white."

"But I don't look as good in white as Marianela does...I want to wear pink or yellow..."

Pins in her mouth, Dona Thomasita ignored the younger girl's complaints and fitted the prized wedding gown to Marianela's young, slim body.

Not long afterward when Antonio arrived for his visit, he and Marianela sat holding hands on the banco by the fire in the sala de recibo. They were allowed the privacy of being alone together—in the house—at this stage of their courtship. They talked of the wedding.

"Bernardo, Alfonso and Francisco all want to be my best man," Antonio laughed. "I told them I couldn't have three...the oldest, Francisco, would be quite enough!"

"Bernardo and Alfonso are just jealous. It's the same with Rebecca, Gloria and Ofelia. Each has asked who gets to walk behind me...first. And they want to know why Rafaela gets to be maid of honor," Marianela said. "But, Antonio! You should see my wedding dress."

"I would like to. Where is it?"

"Oh, you can't...not until the day we are wed. Mother wouldn't approve. She keeps it locked up!"

"Locked?"

The pair laughed and continued to talk about the little things so important to them. Realizing the hour was getting late, Antonio held his bride-to-be closer and whispered, "Sometimes I wish we could have a small wedding ...right here in your family chapel...not such an event. And better, if we could have been married the day after my parents asked for your hand. I hate this waiting...this fuss."

Marianela, amused, pretended to be shocked. "That would be quite improper, sir. What would the neighbors think?"

"I can dream, can't I?"

"But can you wait...thirty-seven more days, not counting Sundays?"

"That long? Ah!" Antonio expelled his breath in mock despair. "Well, my love, I will wait. I would wait forever to have you by my side."

Marianela nestled against him.

"I am yours forever. Our love will be eternal. I know it will," and she let her fingers glide over his cheek to touch his lips while, with an impish glint in her eyes, she looked into his and said, "I don't want to wait forever."

Antonio bent to kiss her on the lips.

Marianela reproved, "Right now, I can hear my father coughing and stirring about in the next room."

They laughed again, knowing well the signals sent by the observing parents. "It seems I've only been here a moment," Antonio lamented as he kissed Marianela once more and bade her goodnight. He chuckled, "Soon we'll be masters in our own home and we'll tell our parents when they visit: 'Now it's time for you to go home.'"

"The snow's almost melted," Francisco announced happily one morning as he and Antonio left the hacienda after breakfast.

"Has been for a week now...except on the peaks," Antonio answered.

And that morning as the brothers rode out with the other vaqueros to see about the cattle, Antonio noted the willows along the streams were pink, bursting in bud. When he and the other riders forded the river, swollen from winter run-off, the water seemed to be singing as it cascaded down from the high mountains. He smiled to himself as he noted tinges of light green along the stream's edge...water cress...wild celery...wild onions. He knew in only a few days he would be wed. *My father says it's been a short, mild winter. But this is the longest winter I can remember.* He recalled other words of his father's: *All signs are for a good spring. Wildflowers are plentiful, new grass has a good start and it will cover the basin, even the mesas this year.*

Always with his eye to the weather and seasons, Don Miguel the good rancher watched for the timing of new calves and lambs. He ordered his vaqueros to ride out daily to assist any cows having trouble calving and he sent his pastores to drive the herds of sheep closer to the lambing sheds so expectant ewes could find shelter against a surprise snow—so common in that country until the last day of May.

"I've seen two feet of snow fall after the middle of May," Don Miguel often was heard to caution his men—so often, in fact, they were heard to imitate him to each other in jest—naturally out of earshot of the patrón.

Another morning, Antonio told Francisco, "I'm stopping at Marianela's. Perhaps her father will allow her to ride along with me."

"You may ask for Marianela but you'll get one of her sisters to boot, you know!" Francisco replied sagely.

"One can't have everything!" Antonio reined his horse toward Don Crescencio's rancho. "Besides, my girl and I haven't been out riding since last fall. It'll do her good to get out."

"You're such a martyr!" Francisco taunted as he watched his brother spurring Chula.

Antonio felt inside his coat pocket to be certain he'd brought the poem he wrote that cold winter night. *I mustn't forget to give it to her.* He'd waited for a day such as this to present his love poem. "Calm down, Chula!" His horse was particularly frisky that morning, rearing her head as she smelled the first blades of grass.

Antonio patted her neck affectionately. "Tired of dry hay? Want to taste some new grass? Well, later, when Marianela and I are walking together, you can graze. You can nip all you can find, Chula."

Soon horse and rider entered Don Crescencio's puertón. There was no one in the courtyard to greet him. Antonio dismounted hastily, threw the reins over a hitching post, ran to the door and knocked. Within seconds, Emma opened the door although it seemed like an hour to Antonio.

Emma stood before him blocking the way, elbows akimbo, scowling. "Well! What brings you here so early or did you forget to leave last night?"

Antonio ignored the unkind accusation. He said courteously, "What a beautiful day, Emma! You certainly look a part of it. May I speak to Marianela?"

Emma couldn't restrain a slight smile at his flattery but she immediately reverted to her tough self and replied tartly, "As with all refined ladies, Marianela is breakfasting with her sisters and mother at *this* hour."

She made it clear this was not an hour to call upon a young lady.

"And why aren't you working? Your father must have much for you to do. Why aren't you doing it instead of disturbing people?"

"There are some things one must do for the soul. Don't you agree, Emma? I came to see if Marianela could go riding with me."

"Humph!" With that she shuddered and looked past him. "I would say no. It's much too cold yet. But you will have to ask her mother, not me." She let him into the kitchen; there she announced in a loud and condescending voice, "There's someone looking for breakfast, Dona Thomasita."

She expected to see some itinerant worker, but instead Dona Thomasita met the gaze of her future son-in-law. "Oh, Emma! You are...terrible," she called, beckoning Antonio to the table. "Welcome, Antonio!"

"Buenos días, Dona Thomasita," he greeted, his eyes on Marianela. "I hope I am not disturbing you unduly."

"Well, it is a little early. I'm afraid you've not caught us looking our best," Dona Tomasita told him, a hand at her hair to see if she had combed it properly. "Here, sit! Emma, pour Antonio some coffee."

"Gracias, señora. I will thank you for a cup but I did eat at home before leaving." The latter remark was intended for Emma.

"Why, just before you entered, we were discussing the color of rugs you should have in your house. Marianela disapproves of the ones we're weaving.

She says there is too much black in them."

Ofelia and Rafaela giggled. Marianela blushed. But from the benevolent smile on the mother's face, Antonio knew it was not a matter of significance at all, only a family game.

"And it's not only rugs, she's so bossy...it's 'don't forget this, don't forget that,' 'do this, do that.' Isn't it, girls?"

The sisters nodded agreement and there was a fresh round of laughter.

"And if we don't agree with her, Marianela resorts to: 'I must discuss it with Antonio!'" Rafaela threw back her head in an imperious fashion, imitating her sister. Marianela blushed again as her sisters and mother had another laugh at her expense.

"Are you really that horrible, Marianela? Perhaps I should know before we marry," Antonio said facetiously.

"I'll get even with them some day...when my sisters marry," she retorted, playing out the game. Then, she reached and took Antonio's hand. "It's so good to see you. Do you know this is the first time I've seen you so early in the morning?"

"You must wonder why this surprise call, señora. It's a grand day...I couldn't resist coming by on my way out to ask if Marianela might accompany me. Wonderful day for a ride," he grinned.

Dona Thomasita replied," Isn't it rather cold to be out riding...I mean for Marianela?" She looked at her daughter for an answer and saw a smile of acceptance on Marianela's face. "I suppose the girls need to get away from the hacienda for a change. We've been cooped up all winter. And it'll give me a chance to do some things I need to do alone. Well, girls...dress warmly. Take your woolen scarves..."

Rafaela complained, "Mama! We don't all have to go, do we?"

"Rafaela! Think of what your father would say."

"I don't want to go. It's no fun," Rafaela insisted.

"Then Ofelia will go. I'm sure you understand, Antonio?"

"Certainly, señora."

Dona Thomasita sighed as the sisters excused themselves. "Sometimes girls are difficult. Boys are much easier. Well, it will be a fine day for a ride."

"Thank you for letting Marianela go with me, Dona Thomasita," Antonio said as he excused himself to see about the horses for the two girls. In the corral, when Cara Linda trotted to him, he was delighted to see how sleek the animal was after the hard winter. "Marianela's been feeding you well, hasn't she?" he remarked patting the horse's neck. "And you're a smart one, aren't you? You remember me after all these months."

In a few minutes, Marianela and Ofelia came to the corral. Antonio helped them mount and the three rode off, but as they passed under the puertón, a strange sensation came over Antonio. He shuddered as if overcome with a strange chill. *My body doesn't feel like "me!"* he thought. But then the peculiar feeling vanished as quickly as it had come over him.

"Look, Antonio!" Marianela said pointing to the color in a grove of tamarisk. "The trees are full of buds."

"It's our world today," Antonio said.

Ofelia rode in silence listening to their enthusiasm wondering if she, too, would feel the same joy at being alive one day.

"Can we ride to that stream we went to last year?" Marianela asked.

"You mean where Antonio took his famous bath?" Ofelia laughed.

"I'd love to go again, Antonio. Let's welcome spring there, shall we?"

"Let's go wherever your heart desires," Antonio said as he rode alongside Marianela. Ofelia was now a little distance in front of them and he discreetly whispered, "I've never seen you so beautiful."

"It's just the wind making my cheeks red."

"I've waited all winter for today!"

"I, too, my love."

"Seeing you...being with you, is the best gift spring could give me. I love you so much." He remembered. "I have something for you," he said and took out a slip of paper from his pocket.

"It's a poem!" Marianela was delighted. "When did you write it? Today?"

"Last winter...a dreary, snowy, cold day when all I had to keep me warm was the thought of you. It's a springtime poem. I wanted to give it to you on our first spring outing."

"Let's stop under that big pine tree so I can read it. I love the view over there anyway...you can see so far."

Antonio helped Marianela dismount, holding her in his arms before setting her feet on the ground. "This is my favorite spot, too. I often ride here to think...dream of us," he whispered.

Ofelia reined her horse, turned and came up to them. "I'm going to ride over to the next hill and wait for you," she said. "Don't worry about me. I'm just going over there to see some prairie dogs I know. Should have new babies by now." With a chuckle, she wheeled her horse and was off at a trot.

Chaperone out of sight, the two lovers fell into each other's arms. Their lips touched, time stopped. They were together, lost in their embrace.

Then Marianela took Antonio's hands and held him at a distance. "Dear Antonio! It will only be a few days and we will be together forever...alone. I'd better read your poem now."

Regaining her composure, she began to read it aloud. As she finished, her eyes were full of tears. She trembled from the emotion his words evoked. "This is the most magnificent poem I've ever read, Antonio. Oh, you are such a romantic. And you make me so happy. I'm so lucky you're a person who gives of himself...you give of your feelings. I ask myself sometimes, if I even deserve you."

"Marianela..."

"This poem will be our song. We'll sing it for lovers everywhere. Forever! I'll treasure it. I love you my Antonio. For all the little things you do...the way you make me feel. Only you can make me feel the way I do right now... so complete...so loved. Thank you for your gift, and thank you for being you." Marianela threw her arms around her beloved and kissed him on the mouth. But their love-making was quickly interrupted by Ofelia's call.

"Hey, you two! Come on! My friends aren't home...some gophers said they'd moved across the river."

Back on their horses, they went off to join Ofelia. Marianela laughed, "That sister of mine! Let's race to see who catches up with her first."

Cara Linda took the lead, then Chula...they then were neck and neck, racing until, without warning, Chula's left front foot sank deep into a prairie dog hole. She tumbled wildly, whinnying in pain; Antonio was thrown fast and hard over her neck. As he hit the ground, he called out "Marianela!" then he lay on his back in silence.

With difficulty, Marianela turned Cara Linda back to the fallen horse and rider.

Unaware at first that Antonio was unconscious, she cried out, "Are you all right? Are you hurt? Antonio!"

Then she leaped to the ground and gently placed his head on her lap.

Ofelia rode up at a gallop. "I can't believe it! It happened so fast! Is he all right?"

Struggling to her feet, Chula managed to stand and limped over to her prone master and tried to nuzzle him.

Antonio moaned but did not speak nor open his eyes.

"Can you hear me, Antonio? Can you speak?" Marianela said choking back her tears.

"Chula must have stepped in a gopher hole." Ofelia sat by her sister and Antonio.

"It's hard for him to breathe! Ofelia...what shall we do?" Marianela burst into tears; a trickle of blood came from Antonio's ear.

"Oh, dear God! What shall we do?" Ofelia cried as she tried to wipe away the blood.

"Ofelia, ride to the hacienda. Fast! Tell father Antonio is hurt badly. Please Ofelia...ride as fast as you can and hurry back with help."

Ofelia made the sign of the cross and was quickly on her horse galloping toward home. As she rode, she thought, *There's always someone we meet as we ride over this section of the rancho...why not today?* She arrived at the hacienda in half an hour. Luckily her father and brothers were coming in for lunch and without dismounting she shouted, "There's been an accident! Antonio's horse fell and he's hurt...I don't know how bad he is. He's bleeding...unconscious. Oh, papa! Help him! Please hurry!"

"Where is he?"

"By that big pine...the lone tree on the hill where you can see in all directions," Ofelia said pointing to the northeast.

"Get the carriage," Crescencio ordered one of his servants. "And, you, Alfonso! Ride to tell Don Miguel to meet us at that pine tree. Bernardo, you'll ride with me!"

Alfonso dashed away on his pony, Don Crescencio and Bernardo rode quickly out of the courtyard toward the scene of the accident.

Ofelia stood in the cloud of dust the horses raised. "I must go in and tell mother," she said.

Don Crescencio and Bernardo rode swiftly to where Antonio lay. Crescencio knew the spot well for he often went there to be alone to meditate. As they approached, Marianela cried out, "Oh, papa! Thank God you've come! I've been waiting forever. Antonio's badly hurt. He doesn't open his eyes. He doesn't speak...he just moans." She caressed his brow and she prayed, "Oh, my Lord, help him!"

Crescencio and Bernardo knelt beside her. The father tried to reassure the girl. "Now Marianela, let me look at Antonio. Perhaps it isn't as bad as you think." He felt Antonio's pulse, leaned down and listened to his chest.

"His breathing is slow. But I can hear his heart beat."

Crescencio touched Antonio's cheek as he spoke: "Antonio! Can you hear me? Antonio?"

There was no response. Crescencio raised one of Antonio's eyelids, then the other. "His pupils are dilated."

"Blood was coming from his ear." Marianela said as she wiped at the dried blood with her handkerchief.

Don Crescencio felt Antonio's head. "I don't feel any knots...no sign of a bruise anywhere. Did he land on his head?"

"I don't know, papa. It happened so fast...I was a little ahead of him when he fell. All I heard was him calling me...call my name. It was the last word he spoke."

Don Crescencio stroked Marianela's brow. "You must be brave, my dear. Antonio is young...strong. I'm sure he will be all right. Here! Let us loosen his belt and take off his boots, Bernardo. Let me get that blanket from my horse to keep him warm. This damp ground isn't good for him to lie on. And it would be better to let him lie without his head propped up, Marianela. He will breathe easier."

They wrapped Antonio in a blanket and waited for him to regain consciousness. Marianela sought comfort in her father's protective arms and she began to cry. "Now, now. The carriage will be here soon and we'll take him to the hacienda. Your Antonio will be fine..."

"What do you think it is, father?" Bernardo asked fearfully.

"A slight concussion, son. It happens sometimes with a hard fall. I've seen several...all recovered. Why don't you take a look at Chula? She seems to have been injured..."

"She has a swollen left foot," Bernardo said as he examined the horse. "I don't think it's broken."

"Can she stand on it?" the father asked.

"She can, but she favors it...she'd rather not, would you, old girl?" Bernardo said and he patted the horse affectionately.

Marianela's attention was on Antonio. "We were having such a great morning, papa. Antonio was so happy...and then this had to happen. Why? Why to Antonio? He is so good, papa."

"I know. I know he is good," he answered looking into the distance, wondering what was keeping the men with the carriage. *I hope Thomasita and the girls stay at the house*, he thought. *We don't need any more weeping out here.*

Marianela cried out in surprise. "Look! He opened his eyes. He's trying to move his arms. Antonio! Can you hear me? It's Marianela. Can you see me? Speak to me, my dearest."

Antonio's eyes were open only a few seconds. He mumbled something incomprehensible, closed his eyes and lay perfectly still. Marianela's tears fell steadily on the blanket.

"There's the carriage!" Bernardo called. A cloud of dust arose in the distance. The rattle of the approaching carriage and the pounding of hooves were welcome sounds to the two men and the heartbroken girl.

"Lift him gently," Don Crescencio said. "And keep him wrapped in the blanket. He should be kept as warm as possible. Is there another blanket in the carriage?"

"Yes, papa," Bernardo answered and swiftly placed it over Antonio.

Marianela said: "Please take Cara Linda, Bernardo. I want to ride with Antonio in the carriage." Then the saddened entourage started slowly toward the Salas hacienda.

Although Marianela kept trying to coax some response from Antonio, there was none. She prayed, "Oh, my God! My Blessed Mother! Please hear my plea. Give me back my Antonio, I beg. I will never ask for anything else again. Make him well, I pray."

As the carriage and the horsemen entered the courtyard, Don Miguel and Francisco rode in. "How is my son, Crescencio?" Miguel called. The two men's eyes met; Don Miguel knew from the expression on his old friend's face Antonio's condition was serious.

Francisco helped carry Antonio into the house. Marianela threw herself into Miguel's arms and sobbed. They walked in silence behind the litter into the house where Dona Thomasita and Marianela's sisters waited at the door.

"I've prepared a room for him. In here!" Thomasita spoke, her face pale with worry.

Looking closely at Antonio, Don Miguel was shocked. "He seems to be in a coma!" As the men placed Antonio on the bed, Miguel sat beside his son and touched his face.

"Can you hear me, Antonio? Can you open your eyes?" He felt his pulse and listened to his heart beat. "His breathing is steady but very slow."

"I found no signs of bruises on his head, Miguel," Crescencio said. "But he did bleed...from his ear."

Dona Thomasita signaled the girls to leave the room with her as the men removed Antonio's clothing and placed him under the bed covers. Don Miguel moved Antonio's arms and legs. "No sign of broken bones," he said with relief. "It must be a concussion."

"That's what it seems to me," Don Crescencio added. "My wife has some coffee ready. Why don't we go to the kitchen, Miguel, while Francisco bathes Antonio?"

Over coffee, Don Miguel asked Marianela and Ofelia about the accident.

"I didn't see him fall, Don Miguel," Marianela answered.

"I did," Ofelia offered. "They were racing toward me. But it all happened in a second. Antonio was pitched to the ground when Chula stumbled."

Dona Thomasita gasped. "I've warned you about racing in the fields, Marianela!"

Marianela went pale. "I didn't think...I'm sorry. It is all my fault. I asked Antonio to race me," she cried, covering her face with her hands and running out of the room. Her sisters began to cry.

"Enough! This is not a funeral." Don Crescencio reprimanded.

In a softer voice, their mother said, "Go to the kitchen, girls, and help Emma prepare dinner. She needs you." As she dismissed them, Dona Thomasita turned to Don Miguel. "Does Rosamaria know?" she asked.

"There was no time. Francisco and I rode here as soon as Alfonso brought the news. And, then, I didn't want to alarm her...I didn't really know what to tell her..." Miguel signed. "But now she must know."

"Send for her, Miguel!" And to both Miguel and her husband, Dona Thomasita implored, "We must send for Martina, the curandera. She will know what to do for Antonio."

The two men nodded in agreement. Francisco entered the kitchen.

"Marianela is sitting beside him now," he said.

"Any sign he is conscious?" Miguel asked.

Francisco shook his head.

"He did open his eyes once...and spoke," Don Crescencio offered reassuringly. "While we were there in the field."

"You must ride to the village, Francisco, and tell your mother. Try not to alarm her. This will not be easy for her. Have the carriage readied and bring her and Martina. Tell Martina I will pay her well for her trouble," Don Miguel instructed his son.

"Here is some bread...and meat to stave off your hunger, Francisco," Dona Thomasita said and she brought food for him and put her hand on his arm. "Tell your dear mother that I'm certain our beloved Antonio will be all right..."

That afternoon, Marianela kept her vigil by Antonio's side. She held her beads in her lap and repeated her rosary over and over. She knew his mother and the curandera would be there any moment and she kept a watchful eye out the window for their approach. Once when she thought she saw the carriage in the distance, she went to the window. "That is not they... it's only that old clump of trees," she murmured.

Then she turned again to Antonio's bed and she saw him open his eyes.

He spoke but his words were barely audible. "Where am I? I should be out with my plants."

He looked directly at Marianela yet he didn't seem to know her. He asked, "Who are you? What are you doing to me?"

Marianela answered with as much composure as she could gather. "You are at our hacienda, Antonio. Chula stumbled and threw you. You're all right, my love. Rest, and you'll be fine again." She bent to kiss his forehead.

Dona Thomasita, Rafaela, Ofelia and Emma came into the room. Antonio blinked at them and said. "Who are all these people?"

He turned impatiently to Marianela. "Who are you?"

Marianela looked at her mother and shook her head.

Antonio said, "I am tired. Please allow me to rest. When I awaken I will leave." He sank back into oblivion, his breathing deep and heavy.

"He doesn't know any of us," Marianela whispered, "Not even me."

"Martina will help him." Dona Thomasita said. "Come, dear. You must get some rest. I will sit with Antonio. There is nothing more we can do until Martina arrives."

But Marianela refused to leave. "I want to stay by his side, mama."

"Then I'll start preparing something for Antonio's family and Martina to eat. Come, girls." They left Marianela with Antonio. The girl's hand rested on his arm and her lips moved feverishly in silent prayer.

In an hour Dona Rosamaria and her daughters arrived, Martina accompanying them. The men waited for them and, as Dona Rosamaria got out of the carriage and rushed into her husband's arms, she saw in his face that all was not well. "Where is he? How is he, Miguel? Tell me he isn't..."

"I believe he will be all right, my dear. He had a blow to his head but there's no visible wound...It's his memory. He's spoken to us. But now he is sleeping," He turned to Martina. "Please go to my son, Martina. Tell us what is to be done."

Dona Thomasita took Dona Rosamaria and Martina to Antonio's room, but after a few seconds, Martina insisted they leave her alone.

"You must go with your mother, too, Marianela," she said.

After they left, Martina spoke to Antonio. He didn't respond. She then anointed him with herbal powder from a small medicine bag. In a few minutes, he opened his eyes, mumbled incoherently and fell asleep. Martina used another herbal, a liquid, which she placed on his lips and tongue. This roused him quickly.

"What are you doing to me? Who are you?" he asked in alarm and tried to get out of bed.

"It is I, Martina, you know me. Don't try to get out of bed. I've come to help. You were thrown from your horse. I want to see where you are hurt." Her voice calmed him and he became less apprehensive. "Now, try to move your leg," she said and he complied. "The other. Good! Can you sit? Easy. That's fine. Tell me, do you feel any pain?"

Antonio looked directly at her; a smile was on his strained face. He said suspiciously, "Kind lady, I feel you are a healer, one who could help me if I needed help. But I must be honest, I have never set eyes on you before. God bless you for trying to help me. I feel so...tired."

Martina was experienced with memory loss so she was not taken aback by his condition. *His memory will return soon,* she said to herself and repaired to the sala de recibo to tell both families of her findings.

"My friends," she said. "I find Antonio's body intact, but the blow to his head was of such force and at such an angle that I believe it caused a clot on his brain and it is this that is causing the memory loss. I think with herbal medicine, and time, the problem will remedy itself."

How long, Martina?" Dona Rosamaria said.

"Not long if we all help him...but not with tears and questions, only with patience and love. I'll provide the herbs."

"When can he go home?" Don Miguel asked.

"When he's rested. But, I caution you, be understanding until he regains his memory. I don't believe he'll recognize any of us for a time."

Marianela cried: "You mustn't say that, Martina. Antonio must recognize me! He will! You'll see!" She rushed from the sala into Antonio's room and flung her arms around him.

Waking with a start, he stuttered, "Wha...? What are you doing? What do you want?"

"It's Marianela, Antonio! You recognize me, don't you, my love?"

He held her at arms' length, looked into her face but his expression remained blank.

"You must remember... Please! We're to be married...remember? It is I, Marianela! Oh, tell me you know who I am...say you are fine," she begged.

"Marianela! Such a nice name," he said dreamily. "But I don't know you, lovely lady. I'm sorry, you must be mistaken... If I had met you, I would remember..." His voice trailed away and he eased himself back on his pillow and went swiftly to sleep.

Marianela stifled her tears until she returned to the sala. Martina tried to comfort her to no avail and at last, her mother took her to her room where Martina prepared a special tea to help her sleep.

For several days, Antonio remained at Don Crescencio's hacienda. When his father and mother thought he was well enough to travel home, they came in the carriage to return him to his own bedroom where he could recover at his leisure.

Dona Rosamaria held his hand as they travelled the familiar road. Antonio stared out at the still-wintery landscape, speckled here and there with green. *They say we are going home. If, indeed, I were, I should know the way. But I've seen none of this before... Ah! The anil del muerto, the cornilla, the dormilon. Now, I've seen them. Strange, but I feel one with them as if I have lived among them. The whole thing is like some sort of dream. I'll wake up soon, surely.*

He closed his eyes. Sleep did not come. Instead, vague thoughts came to his mind: He was walking along a small stream, gathering plants and as he stopped to pick one, he heard it say, "You loved me once. You will again."

When Don Miguel's carriage reached the village, people lined the road, silently and solemnly, hoping to catch a glimpse of their beloved Antonio. The carriage entered the courtyard and Don Miguel turned to face his son, "Home, Antonio."

Antonio looked about. He saw the large hacienda within whose extensive walls there was a village within a village...corrals, blacksmith shops, work sheds, storage sheds, rooms for servants and guests...the hornos, wells, gardens and orchards. But none of it looked familiar.

"You must smile...wave to our people, Antonio. They won't understand your not greeting them. They, too, have been most concerned about your welfare. They love you and welcome you home," Miguel told him.

"But I don't know any of these people," Antonio said. "Surely, they've taken me for someone else. Do I have to speak to them?"

Seeing her son's bewilderment, Dona Rosamaria felt very sad and wanted to cry, but she remembered Martina's words of caution. She told her husband, "He's had a tiring ride. Why don't you take Antonio to his room, Miguel?" Then she went swiftly to the family chapel to pray.

"I'll leave you to rest, Antonio," Don Miguel said closing the door of Antonio's room. The young man looked around him. *Strange room...* he thought as he picked up some rocks on his desk. There were scattered sheets of paper, too. *Poems—love poems!*, and he smiled and brushed his fingers across the words. *Why does everyone call me Antonio?* he wondered. *And why do all these people mistake my identity. I must go away and be alone! Then maybe it will come to me who I am.*

He lay on the bed and closed his eyes. *What is my name?* Juanito came to him. *Why should I think of that name? Juanito! Juanito! Juanito! It's like a cry in the desert. Someone named Juanito is calling me. I must find who this Juanito is.*

When Antonio awoke, he looked up at the ceiling and saw the hanging herbs and plants. He stared at them for some time, then he got up and wandered about the room, lightly touching and caressing the bundles and bouquets. He heard the same words he had heard on the ride to San Lucas. "You have loved us once...you will again."

He shook his head in bewilderment. *They seem to know me...and strange, I feel part of them, too.* Then he said aloud, "Yes, I loved you... I still do." A peacefulness came over Antonio. It was the first time since he came to in the strange room with the beautiful girl that he felt he might belong—somehow, somewhere in this place of all places, which he both knew and did not know.

Don Miguel and his family's concern for Antonio grew. They discussed his condition among themselves frequently. "He doesn't seem to improve, Padre," Dona Rosamaria told the priest who visited San Lucas on his tour of the mission. "The curandera said it would take time, but this long...?"

"You must be very patient and brave. I know your son is in your prayers constantly," the padre said. "With God's will, Antonio's memory will return. He seems to be quite hale in every other respect."

"Except he doesn't have the joy of life he once had, father. He seems preoccupied...not morose, but bothered and pensive. He's not himself. He's not the same Antonio."

"Have you consulted others than Martina?" the padre inquired.

"For weeks, I've summoned all the curanderas and curanderos I can reach near here. Each of them says the same: Only time will tell. One curandera suggested La Concha."

"But Antonio has not been bewitched or cursed!" the padre objected.

"Another said we should consult Juanito," Don Miguel said. "I've not put it out of my mind to seek his help, but as you know, father, the man is strange. Some say he's crazy. I've kept him as a last resort."

"There must be some healer who can help our son." Dona Rosamaria suddenly broke down and wept.

"You must keep faith, my child," the padre said as he blessed them. "Faith in God!"

The days were full of anguish for Marianela. Her family tried to comfort her. "I feel as if I'm being tried," the girl lamented to her mother. "Like Job. But I don't feel strong enough, mother, to go through this ordeal."

"There is a reason for all things that happen in our lives, Marianela, whether they be good or bad. Trust in God that Antonio will regain his memory," Dona Thomasita said.

Days, Marianela let her mind wander through all the wonderful times she had spent with Antonio. Nights, her memories of him before the accident sustained her. She would read and re-read the poems he wrote. Every day she recited the last one he gave her only moments before the horse fell.

"We'll walk hand in hand..." the poem began. But before she ever finished it, she was in tears.

She lived for the days of her visits with Antonio, yet with each visit, her wound was deeper. "There is no change, Marianela," Dona Rosamaria would tell her before each visit. "He simply doesn't remember any of us...we can't expect..."

However, Marianela couldn't resist reminding Antonio each time she saw him that they were to be married. He would smile, then, but the smile was tentative, a gesture made by someone in doubt.

At home Marianela told her mother, "It's the blank look on his face that bothers me so much. I'm glad he's alive, but he's not in our world, mama. He's all by himself somewhere."

On another occasion she told her father, "Antonio and I were to be married next week."

After a long silence, Don Crescencio said, "Don Miguel's doing everything in his power. He's seeking help from healers everywhere."

"He hasn't called on La Concha!" Marianela said harshly.

"Antonio fell on his head. He doesn't need a witch!" Don Crescencio admonished; but as always, he relented, "It is very difficult for us, too, Marianela. We share your hurt and pain. I pray it will soon work itself out and that God will see fit to make Antonio better."

"We will have that wedding yet," Dona Thomasita said confidently.

"But perhaps you shouldn't see Antonio for a while. If fewer people told him who he was and what he was supposed to be feeling, maybe his memory would return without all this prompting."

"I can't stay away from him. He's my life! If I don't see him and remind him, he will surely forget all about me."

"He's not only forgotten you, but all of us. I know what he means to you, but will it help if you keep bothering him? If you could only start all over...fall in love all over again!"

"Anything is worth trying," Don Crescencio said.

"I thank you for your concern and help. I don't wish to sound ungrateful, but if I can't see Antonio and I can't marry him, I will go to the convent in Santa Fe. I'd rather lock myself away than to live without the man I love," Marianela told them.

"It's not the time to make hasty decisions, my daughter. There's so much confusion," Dona Thomasita said.

After Marianela left the room, Don Crescencio said to his wife, "She's so thin. She doesn't eat—no appetite. And I know she doesn't sleep. I hear her crying in the night when I myself can't sleep."

"I hear her too. But what can we do? I feel utterly helpless."

As the weeks passed, Antonio's parents became more desperate. "Time!" Dona Rosamaria sighed. "How much time must we wait? We mustn't leave any stone unturned, Miguel."

"I know. But who else is there? We've asked everyone with any knowledge of healing to help him."

"Juanito!" Dona Rosamaria ventured. "I've heard stories about his powers..."

"I know. But he is inaccessible—living at the top of a mountain. Let's give it more time. Leave Juanito for a last resort."

"Does Antonio talk with you any more than he did?"

"No. He seems more withdrawn. Polite, but he takes no interest. He doesn't seem to care about Chula, and you know how much he set by her. My heart aches for Francisco. The boy can't believe Antonio's affliction."

One morning at breakfast Antonio greeted the members of his family with politeness, but his old affectionate ways were missing. The family tried to engage him in their normal morning conversations, but his silences were deep and troubled. Before the meal was finished, Antonio said, "Dear ones, I would like to tell you something that is bothering me. As you know, I am deeply grateful to you all for caring for me. What I am about to say may sound unfeeling, but I have given it much thought. I wish to leave..."

"Leave?" his mother exclaimed.

"I feel a great need to find someone...a person..."

"Who, Antonio?" Don Miguel interrupted.

"A man named Juanito. From the first day I came to your house, his name has haunted me. I don't know anyone named Juanito, but I hear his name over and over. I feel I must go in search of him. At least then I will have the answer to why I hear his name. Do you know someone named Juanito, Don Miguel?"

"There is a healer who lives on the heights of the Ortiz mountains. Many consider him to have great powers. He seldom leaves his abode. Those who wish his help and wisdom must seek him out. It is a long trek to where he lives," Don Miguel told him.

"Your father and I have already discussed asking Juanito to help bring back your memory," Dona Rosamaria said.

"Then you agree I should leave to find the man?" Antonio asked.

"If it is what you feel you should do. Your horse, Chula, can make the trip. We want to try anything to get your memory back."

"I don't know about bringing back my memory. I only know I get some strange calling to seek this Juanito. I hope he can give me some answers. I thank you, sir and dear lady, for all you've given me. With your permission, I will leave early in the morning."

At the door, Antonio turned and faced them. "If, as you say, you are my parents, I am most fortunate. I hope we meet again some day."

"You speak as if you were not sure of returning to us, Antonio," his mother said sadly.

"I must follow God's will on this journey. I know you understand."

The next morning, Francisco helped Antonio saddle Chula and the entire family saw him off.

"Shall I tell Marianela where you've gone?" Francisco asked as Antonio mounted the mare.

The troubled look returned to Antonio's face. "I hope, if I ever marry," he said, "the girl will be like her. Tell her I go to complete my life."

In leaving, a flood of relief came over Antonio. He guided Chula under the puertón and down the road out of San Lucas. Although he felt appreciative toward the kind people who had nursed him back to health, more than anything he wanted to be alone, to be away from watchful eyes.

Antonio followed the road as Don Miguel had instructed him toward the mountain where Juanito lived.

"What a rich day the night has borne!" Juanito said as he stepped out of his house into the bright, early morning light. A new lunar cycle was just beginning that May and Juanito remembered seeing the date on a man-made calendar. 1881. "Whatever! It isn't important how man marks time, for the seasons will come and go, arranging their own predestined calendar."

From his house, Juanito looked out to the east. He enjoyed a spectacular view from his adobe "temple" atop the Ortiz mountains where he lived alone. Below stretched the Galisteo Basin. Mountain ranges surrounded him. To Juanito, these majestic heights seemed to begin in the basin, taking their origins in the valley, soaring to their craggy heights and touching the sky. Wild creatures abounded in total disregard for any isolated human habitations. There was freedom here for man and beast and the price was understanding the lonely, lovely country.

Juanito, the brujo, the curandero, the man—his role was whatever was needed of him—regarded himself as caretaker of his land. From his lofty perch, he was close to the real powers of the world; from it, he observed all forms of life and bore witness to his God.

Always observant of his neighbors, Juanito noted the small sparrow had added a melodious tune to his winter song. A red ant stuck her head out of the conical pile of sand to feel the sun's rays warming the cold earth. Next door to the ant's home, Satanas, the timber-rattlesnake, moved sluggishly to the entrance of his borrowed winter home—the hole of a poor, dispossessed ground squirrel. All about Juanito there was new movement. Spring!

Juanito smiled when he heard the blind owl calling from a nearby tree. "Tecolote Ciego, my friend and helper," he said aloud. "Your hoot is more songful. You're ready, too, for the new life this fine weather brings."

"I wonder," commented Juanito to himself, "if all the people in the area become as excited as Nature's children when spring finally arrives? But more than that, can they be as grateful as the many plants who have slept for so many months?"

Juanito's plants were his main concern, for his life revolved around their powers. So many people needed the curative qualities of leaf and root—so many people sought them but never found them. Juanito's plants were as alive as he was and whatever he felt, they felt.

Juanito believed that to be born was not always welcome; for just as the child in the mother's womb hesitates at the moment of birth, so the plant is comfortable in the mother. All is serene and beautiful. Who wants to leave this wonderful security? The time to be born arrives or perhaps it is the time to die...Mankind has given these states of being different names. Why, Juanito wondered, should death not precede birth? The child and the plant are pushed into a new state and the cycle goes on. Tecolote Ciego understands I'm sure, but then he has never completed a cycle. His life is to bear witness and impart wisdom. Tecolote has always been and will always be.

Juanito's life was dedicated to people, their physical and spiritual being and all points beyond the soul. His work knew no limits; for him, all people regardless of sex carried unheard-of powers within them. His job was to teach them how they could activate these powers and then use them for their own benefit: good health, a strong mind and, above all, a grateful and thankful spirit to praise God.

Juanito's powers came from God, although he was not active in any religious group. His belief in the Creator and His power was unquestioned since the day Juanito first noticed the unusual powers that were his.

Juanito felt a great need to protect and care for all the Creator's creatures. At first, it was difficult for him to understand what he must do, but in time, the plants and wild creatures spoke to him and he listened until their messages became clear.

He remembered when the Indian paint brush first said to him, "When you find me, Juanito, then see me. I will serve you."

"How must I find you when I already see you," Juanito replied.

"Feel me and speak to me. Be considerate of my space and time. Use me to truly help those in need. Do not barter with me because then you would not have seen me," the plant answered.

Juanito was mystified at first but, from time to time as his understanding deepened, more and more plants and animals spoke to Juanito.

He never understood people in villages using a clock or a calendar to measure time because he observed celestial changes and kept a close eye on his friends, the wild animals all around him. What better measure of a minute than the time it took for a noctural primrose to open its petals with the last ray of sun? An hour was even easier when you observed the patience of a ground squirrel breaking open a pine cone, carefully removing each piñon nut, then scampering to its nest to add to its winter hoard. The movement of the celestial bodies gave him the day and the sun told him the hour.

Life was never lonely for Juanito—so many things needed him. As he sat reflecting on various moments of his life and the compelling work that was his, a strong urge made him turn. Standing in the center of the sunny patio which fronted his small adobe rooms, he saw the old female coyote he'd named Vida. Juanito had found her many seasons ago when she had been orphaned as a pup by her pack. Vida would come and go, but she always remained aloof except for certain times which Juanito had learned to accept.

Juanito named her Vida because she had come to him at a special time when he needed to feel life more than ever: a young man named Pedro had been brought to him on a pine bough stretcher from one of the small villages at the foot of the mountain. Pedro had lost his vision, hearing and was a complete cripple. As always, tears flowed in Juanito's soul when people came to him in such a wasted condition. Pedro's parents were at a loss for words when they arrived with their son. They begged, "Please make him well, Juanito!" That was all the curandero needed, for he had not been confronted with a similar case in a very long time.

Juanito had the boy placed in the work room where he did his healing. This exceptional room imparted great strength and mystery but, above all, it contained Juanito's very soul. As he worked on Pedro, he heard a sad whimper outside his window but he paid no attention and continued on with his chants and prayers.

Suddenly the boy stopped breathing. His face became swollen, disfigured. Juanito used all of his breathing and recovery methods, but none worked. He tried herbal concoctions. Again he heard the forlorn whimper. Looking out the window he saw a young coyote pup. She seemed to want in.

Juanito hollered, "Wait till I bring this young man to life again, pup, then you can enter." But somehow—before Juanito knew it—the pup was inside and licking Pedro's bare feet.

Juanito watched; Pedro began to breathe. "Coyote pup, you have given *vida* to this young man!" Juanito said and then he prayed, "Creator, I accept Your help and I receive Your message with understanding."

The coyote continued her ministrations and Juanito worked right alongside her with his herbal treatment. In a short while, Pedro responded. Juanito turned to touch and thank the pup but she was neither in the room nor was she sitting in the middle of the patio.

"How strange this coyote is, but she is Vida!"

When he was able to walk and to see shadows as well as to hear sounds,

Pedro was delivered to his parents. The family departed after expressing their gratitude to Juanito. "We have a long journey down the mountain, Juanito. Thank God there is such a man as you to do His work," they said.

All that happened some time ago. Now Vida was here again in one of her magical visits. Juanito wondered if this, too, was auspicious. Then he knew it was for a column of dust rose from the north end of Galisteo Basin in the direction of San Lucas.

"Someone is in need of me."

And then Juanito saw a lone figure on horseback.

"I must prepare for our guest."

Late in the afternoon, Antonio could see Juanito's small adobe hut clearly. The sight and smell of the piñon smoke coming from the fireplace cheered him. "Juanito is home," he thought. "I know he is."

As he went up to the dwelling, Antonio noticed how neat and clean it was. In tune with Nature, there were wild plants and birds in abundance. Rabbits—even a coyote—peered at him, unafraid. "What a marvelous place. This person has carved a piece of heaven for himself."

Then a short, stocky man with wavy, brown hair and a handsome, young face appeared.

This can't be the one they call Juanito — he's too young and vital. The Juanito everyone talks about is a man their grandfathers knew.

"Buenas tardes, José. I hope you have had a good journey. Please, come in. My house is yours."

Antonio was perplexed. *Why does he call me José? Is that my real name?* "Are you the curandero called Juanito?" he asked.

"I am."

"I've come to seek your help."

"I know," Juanito said. "You must be tired and hungry. Let your horse loose after you've taken the saddle. She will not stray. Besides, my friends will watch after her." Juanito motioned toward the wild animals scampering about. Antonio did as Juanito said and then followed him into the house which was also trim and neat—harmony seemed to prevail within and without.

"Please sit by the fire and I will brew a cup of warm moradilla tea for us. We will relax before we eat," Juanito said with his pervading air of calm.

When their drink made from the purple verbena was finished, the two began to talk. "You are so close to nature here. You must have found true peace and love up on this mountain, Juanito."

"I am close to God."

"Why did you call me José? In San Lucas they say my name is Antonio."

"The name José came to me. It seems your real name. However, I do not doubt your birth name is Antonio, which is a fine name indeed. But perhaps you can tell me more than I already know about "José"—better yet, we can both find out who you are."

"Are you telling me José is another person within me, someone who takes over for Antonio on occasion? Or is José just a spiritual part of me?"

"I do not wish to confuse you, my young friend. I feel that is one of the reasons you have sought me—because you are confused. So let me put the question to rest by asking you to listen to what I have to say. I will give you back only what you already have but do not know how to use. José, whoever he might be, lies deep within you. Usually he comes forth only in times of great need. Times of sorrow, pain, desperation. You, as Antonio, are unaware that it is he who pulls you through these periods of turmoil. He is that extra strength in the final effort. In time, I foresee you will understand and learn to utilize José more often in your daily life."

Juanito leaned back against the sheepskin pillow and looked at Antonio trying to discern if the young man understood him.

Antonio said, "I have been here only a short while and yet I feel certain I've known you forever. I shall try to understand what you tell me and to be more aware of my José."

"We have much to talk about. First, let me offer you a warm meal," Juanito said and he went to a covered, cast iron kettle hanging in the recess of the fireplace. He served the food on two wooden plates.

"Delicious!" Antonio exclaimed when he took a bite. "What is this in the mutton?"

"Wild onions, watercress," Juanito answered, smiling.

When they had finished, Juanito gave Vida their leftovers.

"I was a bit startled to see a coyote in your patio when I came up to the house. I never knew one that trusted people. She must really care for you."

"All the creatures of the Creator care for us. We must show we care for them." Juanito answered solemnly.

The two talked long into the night. "I am deeply troubled, Juanito. I awoke in the house of Don Salas one day as if I had just been born, not remembering anything of my past. The family of Don Salas as well as that of

Don Miguel Ortiz, which claims me as a son, show every sign of loving me. They are all sincere people. And the girl, Marianela! How many times she told me we were to be married! How is it possible I cannot remember anything of my life and these wonderful people?"

Juanito listened in silence as Antonio poured out his heart. "You remember absolutely nothing?" he said at last.

"Only the plants...I felt I knew them. They were like old friends. I also had the feeling I needed to work with them and this work would eventually help others."

"Tell me what you feel—anything you can remember," said Juanito.

As Antonio talked, Juanito thought to himself: *His knowledge comes from a hidden wellspring deep within. We must not allow him to waste his knowledge... his gift.* To Antonio, he said, "The hour is late. Let's continue our talk tomorrow. The body and mind need rest. Let us sleep. If you wish, you may sleep on the banco next to the fireplace. I will retire to my temple room." Juanito made Antonio comfortable with sheepskin rugs and immediately the young man fell into a deep sleep.

It was still dark when Antonio was awakened by someone chanting. Going to the window, he saw Juanito standing with outstretched arms, praying to the stars. He listened to the prayer:

"Heavenly stars, children of the Creator, thank you for the light that gives me direction. Thank you for the power that helps me heal."

Antonio listened to Juanito's song for that is what it was, and thought, *What a beautiful way to start the day. I want to go out and join him...but, no— perhaps it would be best to wait to be invited. I respect this man more than any other I have ever met.*

In a short while Antonio heard Juanito return to his temple room. He called, "Is it time to get up, Señor Curandero? I enjoy greeting the first rays of the sun."

Juanito came in and looked very much awake and refreshed. He smiled at his guest and said, "Yes. Let us go out together and greet the sun."

They sat outside in silence, each in his own thoughts. The sun appeared over the horizon, turning the Galisteo Basin into a colorful sea of red and orange. Antonio felt the land and air start to stir.

"Do you think the sunrise gives us strength, Juanito?"

"That is a very important question. Few people understand this wondrous moment. The other creatures of the Creator—birds, rodents, plants—

anticipate the sunrise. They plan their days according to what the sunrise reveals."

"What do you mean? How can the creatures plan their days?"

"Well, if the sun rises through low-lying clouds, and is very dark crimson, there is a good chance of rain. So they prepare for rain. If the sun rises in fog or mist, chances are it will be a clear day. And so it goes. You can learn much from a sunrise," Juanito replied.

"I never tire of listening to you, Juanito. You are truly a great teacher. I want to be as wise as you and help people with their problems as you do. I feel I've done it before, although I can't remember when. Perhaps in another life? I do believe in the Creator's plans and their powers. Teach me the proper way to utilize the power of the plants, Juanito."

"I believe you are devoted to this study, José. I will call you José to remind you of the special power within you. But you must use the name Antonio until you discover the other self whom you still have not met. I will teach you to find him. You must give yourself totally to the quest of using herbs to help people. It will not be easy for there are many things you have to learn. You must look at plants, feel them, listen to them grow. All plants are aware of their purposes. If we trust in them and respect them, they in turn will help us."

"I trust you. And I shall try not to disappoint you. I will give myself totally," Antonio answered.

That day marked the beginning of a two-year course in which the student faithfully served and eagerly learned what the master taught.

Marianela seldom smiled those days after Antonio left on his quest. Some months after he had gone, Don Miguel announced at a gathering at Don Crescencio's that he and his wife intended to visit their son. Marianela begged to accompany them—her parents consented.

During the family gatherings, news of Antonio was always eagerly sought but there had been none other than "He's still at Juanito's"..."He's studying"..."He's in good health." So with the approaching visit, Marianela's spirits rose. Her parents and family were delighted to see the gloom begin to disappear. She was her old self again.

However, her mother tried to warn her of undue expectations. "If Antonio's memory had returned, he himself would have returned."

"When he sees me, he'll remember mama! I know he will."

Early one morning that summer, Don Miguel, Dona Rosamaria, Francisco, Rebecca, Marianela and two of Don Miguel's vaqueros, set out to visit Antonio.

"We are going to set up camp near Juanito's and spend a few days visiting," Miguel told Crescencio.

"I only hope that Antonio's memory is all right. I cannot imagine how Marianela will live if he doesn't remember her..."

From their perch atop the mountain, Juanito and Antonio saw the group making its way slowly toward them.

"Who are they...there must be six or seven in the group," Antonio said. "Usually only one or two come to see you at a time."

Juanito was quiet for some time before he answered, "I feel they are some of your loved ones in search of the old Antonio. It is important how you receive these people, José. Come, let us gather firewood. We must prepare for their visit."

When Don Miguel's entourage stopped half a mile away, Antonio was surprised. "Look! They are making camp."

"They intend to remain a few days. That is fine," Juanito answered.

"But, why?"

"They are concerned about you. They hope you recognize them...that your memory has returned," Juanito said, adding: "There is something I wish to tell you now. Not once have I told you or led to you believe that you are who they say you are when we speak of your problem."

"That's true," Antonio answered. "What is it you wish to tell me?"

"I have known you since you were a child. It is true you are the son of the family which claims you. You are Don Miguel Ortiz' elder son, his heir."

Antonio gasped in disbelief. As he looked into Juanito's unbeguiling eyes, he knew the curandero spoke the truth. "Why have you waited until now to tell me?"

"There was no reason before. I waited for the José within you to heal...to return your memory. I tell you this now—a word of advice—to caution you to be loving toward them. Accept them."

"How can I when I don't recall one little event..."

"It is not wise to sweep the trail clean behind you."

"Sometimes I don't understand what you tell me."

"Do not lose faith."

"I will do as you bid. I cannot find it in my heart to hurt anyone who has helped me," Antonio said with a sigh.

The next day when the visitors arrived, Juanito greeted them. "Welcome to my humble home! It is yours." Antonio stood beside him.

"My son!" Don Miguel called rushing to greet Antonio with an abrazo.

Marianela threw herself into Antonio's arms. "Antonio! My Antonio. It's so good to see you," she cried with tears in her eyes.

The embarrassed Antonio tried to disengage himself by saying: "It is good of you wonderful people to come this long distance to visit me."

"Don't pull away from me, my dearest," Marianela implored. "You remember now, don't you? It's been so long..."

"I remember how kind and gentle you were when I was at your home," he answered.

"Nothing else...before the accident?" she cried.

"Nothing. I'm sorry." Antonio turned as if to leave the guests. He wanted to run away but he remembered Juanito's words of caution.

"Let us all go into the house," Juanito quickly invited.

Once settled inside, an awkward mood fell over them. None knew how to start the conversation. Don Miguel finally said, "We have set up camp a short distance from your home, Juanito, that we might visit with you the next few days."

Juanito answered with a nod of his head.

Dona Rosamaria turned to Antonio. "You may visit with us there when you wish."

"Thank you, dear lady." Antonio replied.

Marianela had difficulty maintaining her composure. *I love him. I will wait forever. Oh, Antonio! give me some little sign that you still care*, she thought.

Juanito said, "We have been studying. Antonio wishes to be a curandero. The best! He has devoted all his time and effort to pursuing this study. I am proud to say, the Almighty willing, soon He will have another loyal servant." Juanito beamed proudly at Antonio. Then he said to the others, "I feel, in time, when he heals others, Antonio will heal himself."

Later, when alone with Don Miguel, Juanito shook his head in reply to the father's questions. "There has been no change in his memory. When you are ready to leave, return to your home, continue to pray for him, hold him close to your hearts, never lose faith. When the time is right, he will return to you."

Antonio's loved ones remained two days. In parting he told them, "Beautiful people, I shall never forget you."

To Marianela he said, "If what you say should have been between us, it shall be. Our destinies can't be changed by either of us."

"And you? What will you do until that time?"

"I'll remain with Juanito until he feels I am ready to go forth and heal those who need me."

The saddened group wound its way down the mountain—their only solace the knowledge that Juanito was doing his best to help Antonio. Marianela's tears fell on the sand and clay of the beautiful basin that lay at the foot of Juanito's mountain.

In the three long years that followed, Juanito taught Antonio to speak with plants and to listen to them speak to him. Juanito also taught him about lunar cycles; how celestial bodies are important in the lives of plants as well as men. He taught Antonio how important it is to develop sensitivity in seeing, feeling, listening to his body. "You must transfer this sensitivity to your hands and fingers so that when you work with people you can feel the blood flowing in a person with your fingers. You must learn to touch various organs of the body such as the liver...feel if any part is sluggish or damaged. You must learn to feel the child's position in the mother's womb."

There were lessons in making herbal oils used to untangle spasms in muscles, tendons and ligaments. No part of the human body would remain a mystery to Antonio, once Juanito finished his teaching.

"So much to learn," Antonio sighed when he tried to sleep at night. *Will I ever know enough to help others—without Juanito? The man is truly gifted by the Creator. How did he acquire such vast knowledge? He must be chosen.*

Juanito always surprised Antonio with new subjects. He taught him the spiritual levels of man and how they influenced his health. And diet, about which Antonio previously had not paid much attention. Exercise..."All are inseparable in dealing with illness. The emotional state of a sick person is important. It must be calmed and centered before you are ready to use herbs in healing. But above all, the healing process depends on the positive attitude of the healer."

"I know your doubts, José. Put them aside. You will eventually retain all I've taught you. You will remember and be able to use this knowledge without thinking someday. And without doubting!" he added. "Don't worry, you are doing well. I notice how gentle you are with the people who come in search of me. It is a fine quality in you."

That evening as they ate, Juanito said in a low voice. "I will send you on your way soon."

"Leave!" Antonio exclaimed.

"Let us go out and sit while I tell you of your first quest you make as a curandero...alone." Juanito stretched his hand to the west. "There is an old mining village in that direction, on the other side of this mountain. It was founded by the Spanish who named it Dolores—a name that befits it today because of the problems that have arisen there. There is evil in Dolores. The people have a right to be sad."

"What causes this evil?" Antonio asked, still feeling sad at the thought of leaving.

"A curandero named Carlitos. He has betrayed his people as well as himself. Tragically, the people of Dolores have placed their health in his hands...their very lives. They believe Carlitos is helping them."

"Is he a witch?"

"Yes and no. I will tell you this. When people come for healing, instead of trying to help them, he administers herbs or potions that do them great harm. This has been confirmed by various people who have made the trek here to consult me."

"Is he mad? Can't the people see what he's doing to them?"

"For some time I have suspected Carlitos is a very sick man. Sickness clouds a man's reason," Juanito answered, "it makes him do things he would not otherwise do."

"Where did this man Carlitos come from?"

"He is a self-made curandero whose past life is unknown. By now the people of Dolores are intimidated by him. If they don't do as he says, he threatens them with his unwholesome ways—his dark powers."

"But why?" Antonio asked.

"To gain property...wealth. The unfortunate people of Dolores have granted him all kinds of favors. No one opposes him. Only someone like you could unseat him."

"I?"

"Using the power of your real self, the José, you can vanquish Carlitos. But it will be a dangerous enterprise. Once he suspects you are in Dolores to undermine him, his wrath may be turned on you."

"You believe I can undertake such a mission...?"

"I do, or I would not send you," Juanito replied. "Of course, I will aid you whenever necessary."

"When do you wish me to leave?"

"Before the snow flies."

Although Antonio knew that the day would come when he would have to leave Juanito and his tutelege, he had put the thoughts out of his mind. Now, the time had come. Curious thoughts popped in his mind. Poetry...he started to write poetry.

Why should I turn to poetry now? What has poetry to do with my work with Juanito? And Marianela's face kept coming out of nowhere... Antonio wondered what had happened to the beautiful girl in the years since he last saw her. *Some fine young man married her,* he thought.

On the appointed day of his departure, tears welled up in Antonio's eyes. Juanito said, "This is not a time for tears. Go. You will succeed. Never forget to place our Creator first in all you do. Use humility as your sword. You are like a conquistador...on a special mission."

"When shall we meet again?"

"I do not know, except that our paths must cross again. Of that I am certain."

Juanito watched Antonio mount Chula and ride away over the distant hills. Then he knelt in front of Vida and stroked her neck. "Vida, you always live up to your name. What will you bring me next? I miss Antonio

already. But he has greater things to do, and you and I must remain on the
mountain and send our power to him.

Chula wound her way in and out of canyons, mesas and thick woods of
piñon brush. A cold, harsh wind blew from the north. Antonio saw smoke
rising from the chimneys of Dolores which was tucked away in a pleasant
and picturesque valley. "A fine looking village," he thought. "The homes
seem well-kept. I expected worse from this mining town."

As he guided his horse between the adobe houses, dogs barked at him,
but no one appeared. *Staying close to their fires. I don't blame them,* Antonio
said to himself. At the end of a lane he noticed a store. He stopped to rest
and inquire about lodging after tying Chula to the hitching post and patting
her. "Thanks for the safe ride, Chula, And your patience!"

The cowbell on the door clanged as he entered the store. At first he
thought he was alone in the room, but then a man sitting behind a high
counter spoke. The man was hidden by the shadows of the soft light glowing
from a kerosene lantern.

"Welcome, stranger! Come in by the fire. What can I do for you?"

"I've been travelling all day, señor. My horse and I could use shelter for
the night. Can you make any suggestions?" Antonio answered, warming his
hands by the fire.

"I think we can arrange that. Will you be staying more than one night?"

"I hope to stay longer if I can find a room or two. My name is Antonio,"
he said and extended his hand. "I come from San Lucas. I am a curandero."

"My name is Fidel. I am the owner of this store."

"I am happy to meet you."

Fidel looked at Antonio with curiosity. "What brings you to Dolores?
We already have a curandero. Haven't you heard of Carlitos? He takes care
of the people here."

"I practice somewhat differently than Carlitos, so there shouldn't be any
problem."

"I see," Fidel said nervously. "Well, I have a small room at the back I've
been using to store grains. It needs cleaning, but if you wish, you may stay
there until you find something better."

"I appreciate your accommodation, señor. And tomorrow I will clean
the room. I've had an exhausting day...a long ride. If I may buy a few tins of

food, some feed for my horse and a place to put her up, I won't bother you."

Shortly afterward, Antonio fell asleep, wrapped in his blanket in the cluttered room. In the darkness, Fidel hurried off toward Carlito's house.

A shaft of light streaming through a crack in the door awoke Antonio the next morning. The sun had just risen. He stretched and climbed out of bed to prepare for his morning prayers. Something red at his feet caught his eye. Nailed to the door was the bloodstained head of a rooster. The drops of blood on the door were still warm. *Good. Carlitos knows I've arrived.* Antonio said to himself. *No time to waste.*

Antonio finished his prayers before turning to the task of cleaning the room. While he was sweeping, Fidel appeared. "Antonio! Are you all right?"

"Buenos días, Fidel! I am fine. And you?" he asked cheerfully.

"I am fine, but I saw somthing on your door and I wondered what it was about."

"You know very well. You even know who hung it there. That amuses me, Fidel. But I am still grateful to you for use of the room."

"Do you think Carlitos put the chicken there?" the other asked.

"Let's forget about it. Who is the alcalde in Dolores? I would like to let my presence be known to him and to the villagers as well," Antonio said.

"There is no alcalde. The people of the village ask me for advice on any matters of importance," Fidel answered proudly. "Perhaps I can help, if you have something to discuss."

"I intend to remain here and I will help those who have illness. I have finished a three year apprenticeship with Juanito whom you must have heard of. I come to Dolores as a healing instrument of our Creator."

"You won't make a living here," Fidel scoffed. "Our people are poor. The mining has all but stopped. They cannot pay you. They have already lost homes....land...possessions."

"How did they lose these things?"

"Trading for services...food and..."

"...health care? Hasn't Carlitos acquired his wealth in exchange for try-ing to help the sick?"

"I...I suppose so. But Carlitos makes many people well." he stammered.

"We both know the truth about that. But I will not trouble you further. I only ask you to help me meet a few of the villagers. Don't worry about how I survive. The important value is truth. That will be my most powerful medicine. I'll not charge, for if I should, the Creator who has blessed me with the power of healing would strip me of that power. One does not barter with a gift!"

"You are a very strong young man...that I can see," Fidel told him. "Come to my store and spend the day with me. You will meet the villagers as they come in."

"I appreciate your kindness."

In the early afternoon, Antonio went to his room. He was met at the door by a woman with a reboso draped over her head and shoulders.

"Buenas tardes, Señor Curandero! May I have a word with you?"

"Certainly," he replied.

She was a young woman, probably in her twenties, with black eyes that shone as she spoke. "Señor, my name is Yolanda. My father has been very ill for two years. We would be grateful to you if you would honor us with a visit. Although we have tried everything, nothing has helped the poor man. I heard from the neighbors that you have come to Dolores to cure the sick."

"Where do you live?"

"Beyond the church...there on the plaza. My father is Arturo Montoya. Our family has lived in Dolores many years. Everyone knows us."

"And is your father a miner?"

"He spent his whole life searching for gold. Now he is barely alive."

"I will go with you now, if you wish," Antonio told her.

"I was hoping you could see him today. Thank you!"

When they entered the Montoya home, Antonio noted how neat and orderly it was. Yolanda left him in a small entrance hall, then went to the back part of the house. She returned with her mother who offered him a warm cup of chocolate and biscochitos. "Thank you, señora. I have yet to eat today," Antonio said as he accepted the nourishment.

"We are getting my husband ready for you, señor," the mother said and left him with Yolanda.

Antonio noticed how beautiful Yolanda was—her body lithe and delicate, her step light and firm. Suddenly he remembered Marianela. A warm, tingling sensation came over him. He felt his cheeks burn with excitement. Yolanda's younger sister announced their father was ready.

Arturo Montoya was lying on a small, wooden bed. Although he was probably only fifty, he looked almost twice that age. Only his black, piercing eyes seemed to be alive.

"Buenas tardes, Señor Montoya. I am Antonio. I've come to help you if you will permit me."

A feeble voice spoke from the desecrated body. "Gracias! Come closer that I may hear you better."

The women folk left the room and closed the door behind them. "How has your condition come upon you?" Antonio asked.

"It started with a fever several years ago when I worked in the mines. The fever grew worse and my family asked Carlitos for help. He gave me herbal tea and showed my wife how to prepare it. 'You'll be well within a few days,' he said. And within a few days the fever was gone."

"What was this tea?"

"It was made from the roots of the cholla cactus. It seemed to work. I regained my health and went back to work. But within a few weeks it came back. It consumed my strength. My wife called Carlitos again. Then he gave me another herbal tea. It tasted terrible. It was made from the roots of the river willow. It was at that time" the man heaved a long sigh, "when Carlitos told me I must give him all the gold I had in order that his medicine would heal me."

"And did you?"

"Yes. I had some nuggets put away. I wanted this illness to go away more than anything, so I gave them to him, hoping..."

"And you have been like this for two years?"

"I grow weaker each day. I can't eat. Carlitos will soon own my home. We have nothing left to give him. I pray to God you have been sent to help me. I am desperate, Señor Curandero."

"With your help, I will get you well. Our Creator will guide us through this illness."

"I have nothing with which to pay..."

"Don't worry, Arturo. Your health will be pay enough. And do not worry about Carlitos. Once he knows I am working with you, I am sure he won't bother you any longer." Antonio's strength made the old man smile. "Now, I must talk with your people to let them know what has to be done."

Later Antonio returned to his room to select herbs from the stock he had brought from Juanito's. He trembled with excitement. *My first patient!* But a feeling of loneliness crept into his thoughts and travelled from the pretty Yolanda to Marianela. *I mustn't think of her. Not now!* he told himself. *There is much to do to bring that sick man back to health.* As he worked, he remembered the villagers he had met that morning—the looks on their faces.

They hope, but doubt. I'm certain some must have told Carlitos about me by now. I must visit him and explain why I am here. I must see him in order to "feel" him. Tomorrow I'll go to his house.

From his collection, Antonio selected a combination of wild rue and moradilla. These herbs were most powerful; and he selected them because they coincided with the lunar and celestial cycles of that month, week and day. He was following Juanito's teachings exactly.

When Antonio left his room to return to the Montoya home, he passed the church which was in the center of the village. There he saw two large, black dogs which barked and snarled as he approached.

They're half starved, but they act as if someone's prodding them to attack me.

Standing his ground, he spoke softly holding out his hands. "Here, dogs! Do not take your anger out on me!" So saying, Antonio placed himself in a trance that removed his presence from the hostile animals. Although they could still see him, his smell was undetectable and the dogs began to whimper. They placed their tails between their legs and took off in the opposite direction.

After regaining his normal self, Antonio felt exhausted. The reaching within had sapped his strength. *These dogs belong to Carlitos who lives beyond that hill...Tomorrow, he will receive a visitor.*

As he knocked on the door, there was time for a short prayer. "St. Joseph, be with me, give me strength as I attend my first patient."

A handsome, dark-haired young man opened the door. "Come in, Señor Curandero. I'm Manuel, Yolanda's husband. The family is waiting for you."

He's about my age," Antonio thought. *"How lucky to have such a beautiful wife.* Then without intending to, his thoughts turned to Marianela. *It's been so long since I saw her. I wonder if she's forgotten me? I only hope, some day, to find a woman who will be willing to share my life."*

Antonio taught Señora Montoya to prepare the tea from the herbs he had selected and he instructed her when to have Arturo drink them. "Twice a day, señora. And he must have a soup made from fresh liver or kidneys once a day for the first week. Save the blood from the calf or sheep you kill and cook it with a great deal of garlic. Have him eat all he can," he said.

"But my husband has no appetite..."

"After the first two cups of tea, he will grow hungry," he assured her. "And have him drink water as often as you can. I will return in two days or sooner if you need me. You know where I am staying."

As he turned to leave, the woman said, "Please, Señor Curandero. We ask you to partake of our simple dinner."

Antonio gladly shared the pinto beans and salt pork they offered him. Later, when he was ready to leave, he again reassured the family they would see a change in Arturo very soon. "With the will of our Creator, he will be completely cured. Do not lose faith. And pray for Arturo!"

Back in his small room, Antonio wrapped himself in his blankets and fell into a deep sleep. He dreamed of Marianela.

At that moment, Marianela was in her room gazing at the star-filled heavens. She prayed, "Dear God, keep him and protect him. I know Antonio is now a curandero working in the village of Dolores. Grant him to do Thy bidding, but...bring him back to me, I pray!"

She remembered something Antonio had said. "In the clear, cold winter months, the stars reach their heights of splendor and power. You can see them much more clearly. Celestial bodies know most people don't star-gaze on cold, uncomfortable nights. So, the stars reward you when you look at them in winter. They'll reward special wishes."

She repeated a verse she had made up:

Falling star, tell me where you are. Tell me that you care. Show me that you're there. Falling star, bring back my Antonio. She also prayed that in healing others, he would heal himself.

Antonio's family took solace in knowing he was in Dolores, working and healing. Travellers sometimes gave news of him, but the family no longer tried to contact him.

Juanito and Vida hovered near the fireplace that night. "I have been feeling Antonio very strongly these past days. An encounter with Carlitos is imminent," Juanito told Vida as he stoked the fire with a thin cedar stick. It ignited and burned slowly. Reading the message of the curling smoke, Juanito saw a confident Antonio, reaching inside himself and successfully dealing with Carlitos. "We must continue sending our strength to Antonio.

The most trying times for him are yet to come," he told Vida. "We miss him but we have not lost him. He will always be with us. We are one."

Antonio was wakened early the next morning by a loud knock. It was Fidel. "Señor Curandero! I hate to bother you, but you must find another room. I have a load of grain coming. I'll need this room today."

"Why are you so upset?" Antonio asked. "Do you have something else to tell me?"

"Just that."

"Thank you for giving me shelter and for letting me meet the villagers in your store. I will look for another room immediately. But I want you to know that I believe your reason for asking me to leave is because of Carlitos."

"Carlitos has nothing to do with this," Fidel said unconvincingly.

"The truth will be known. I will leave, but I want you to be my friend, Fidel. Don't hesitate to call me if I can ever be of service."

When Fidel hurried off, Antonio said his daily prayers, gathered his effects and herbs and went to feed Chula. Then he saddled and mounted and rode off to meet Carlitos.

On the way past the church, he noticed a plaque. "Santa Lucia!" he exclaimed. "A beautiful name for this church." He then prayed to that most blessed saint whose eyes evil-doers had put out. "Santa Lucia, you who help those who cannot see, help me today so that my eyes may see."

Riding toward the hill where he saw the dogs disappear, Antonio went deep into his mind. "I can feel his presence," he thought. "Juanito, you are with me, assuring me I can correct the evil Carlitos has wrought. I am happy you taught me to fight evil. Even if Carlitos calls upon the devil, himself, I feel strong enough to overcome them both."

He crested the hill. Below him lay a small valley densely covered with cactus and chamisa brush. Centered in it was a large adobe house built in a square with a courtyard in the middle. Something about the scene was foreboding. Antonio decided not to take the path leading to the house but to make his own.

He arrived at the front door unnoticed and knocked. There was an iron clanger in the shape of a human skull—a femur bone-shaped piece of iron next to it served as the knocker. Antonio didn't use them. Instead he pounded on the heavy cedar door with a stick of wood.

After several minutes, two young girls clad only in black muslin pon-chos opened the door. Their faces were strangely alike. They seemed to be dazed. . .perhaps drugged or hypnotized . .or maybe deaf. Then one of them asked, "Who are you? What brings you here?"

"I am Antonio, the curandero. I would like to speak to Carlitos. Are you his daughters?"

The question startled them. "No. We are his disciples," the girl said. "Come in and we will see if Carlitos can see you."

Antonio remained in the large entrance hall. The room was tomb-like with rock floors against mud walls. There were a few pieces of simple wooden furniture in front of the fireplace. The walls were hung with Indian blankets and skins of animals. An eagle's wings stretched over the fireplace. Antonio observed the room while his energy reached for the José within. Ephemeral elements of the negative disappeared; he felt strong and sure.

Then he caught a glimpse of one of the girls watching him from behind a blanket on the wall. Antonio knew that she had been joined by Carlitos who was watching as well. *They are not sure of me,* he thought.

Then one of the look-alike girls entered and beckoned to him to follow her down a narrow corridor. She walked in a peculiar manner. *Carlitos has drugged her. Perhaps tolache,* he thought. She knocked on a door, opened it.

Inside a huge fire burned in a large, bell-shaped fireplace. Kerosene lanterns flickered brightly. Rock floors, adobe walls, large vigas overhead. On a buffalo hide in front of the fire was a tall, ornate chair with its back to the door. The second girl sat by the chair and stared into the fire.

At first, Antonio didn't see anyone else, but then a scratchy voice said, "Greetings, Antonio!"

The girl motioned him toward a chair where a thin, withered man with white hair came toward him and sat in the ornate chair. His feet dangled, not reaching the floor.

Antonio had expected to find a stronger, younger man, not this old, frail lizard of the desert dressed in a white toga, like frayed rags. *Carlitos is creating an illusion,* Antonio thought. He prayed: *Santa Lucia, don't let my eyes deceive me; show me only the truth.*

"So, you are Antonio, the curandero who has come to save the people of Dolores! I must say you are handsome. . .a magnificent body. No wonder my young disciples, Ramona and Christina, are so excited. You have met them: the light haired one is Ramona, the brunette, Christina."

"It is a pleasure to meet you, Carlitos," Antonio said.

Carlitos drew his miserable frame to its full posture. "The people in this area are well attended by me. I have taken care of their needs for many years. We have no need of another curandero. Go somewhere else. You have much to learn. Am I not right, Ramona? Christina?"

The girls answered by nodding mechanically.

"I have reason to believe you are not helping the people of Dolores," Antonio stated. "Only last night I was with a man who is slowly dying. This is your work, Carlitos."

Carlitos' small frame trembled with subdued rage. He pulled himself forward and said hoarsely: "You are foolish! I will not tolerate such an accusation. You are only beginning the life of a curandero. Your experience cannot match mine. I know the man you saw last night. He will not get better with your treatment. He will die. Soon! Then you will see how people scoff at your efforts!"

Carlitos got out of his chair and stood before Antonio. His eyes bore down on Antonio. "I will run you out of Dolores. I warn you. Leave now!" the old man said.

Antonio only looked through him, stared at Carlitos, unmoved.

"I have no fear of you or your power," Antonio began calmly. "I came to pay a visit, to advise you of my intentions. I have no wish to use my power against yours. I only want to do what is right for people who depend on curanderos. If that interferes with your work, so be it. I come in peace. You receive me with threats. I leave your house, but I continue my work."

Suddenly Carlitos laughed. "So you return to your patient. Did you know that Ramona is Señor Montoya's daughter? You have met her sister, Yolanda."

Antonio was taken aback by these words but he didn't answer, he only stared at Ramona.

"Ramona is willing to help you, if you would like to take her with you. I can forgo her services," the old man coughed lewdly.

Although he was incensed at Carlitos' offer, Antonio controlled himself. "You not only take gold in barter, but people! I will not call on you again, Carlitos, you can be sure of it."

Antonio left abruptly.

Outside, the cold air refreshed him. He made his way to the Montoya home, lost in thought.

Yolanda answered the door and he felt the change immediately. "It is good to see you, Señor Curandero. You will be pleased to see how well my father is doing already." She led him to the bedside where Arturo was sitting up, eyes sparkling.

"How are you feeling?" Antonio asked.

Arturo's voice was strong. "For the first time in months, I want to live. And, for the first time I believe I shall get well. I have been following your instructions very carefully."

"You will take your place as the head of your family again, Arturo!" Antonio said firmly.

The others expressed their gratitude and Antonio prepared to leave.

"Do you stay at Fidel's?" Señora Montoya asked.

"I have been asked to leave. I must find another room and a stall for Chula. Do you happen to have a spare shed we might use, Señora?"

"There is a nice shed for your horse and we have a separate room you may use for as long as you wish. It will be an honor for us if you would accept, Antonio."

"I don't wish to take advantage of your hospitality; a shed would suffice for me. My needs are simple."

"Think nothing of it. The room is yours. We won't hear of you sleeping in a shed," Yolanda told him.

With a sudden remembrance of Carlitos, Antonio said: "I only hope Carlitos will not try to do you harm if I stay with you."

"I think that man has done all the harm he is going to do." the señora answered solemnly.

So Chula and Antonio settled in. That night, Manuel gave Antonio a glass of mula before dinner and the group sat about the kitchen talking for an hour or so before Antonio went to his new room.

He lay on the wool mattress thinking, *This is the most comfortable bed I've had since. . .* and his thoughts returned to San Lucas to the hacienda of the man who claimed him as a son, to Dona Rosamaria, to Marianela. He thought of the hard banco he had slept on at Juanito's. *I wonder if Marianela, or any woman, could accept the life I must lead. . .poor. I mustn't think of Marianela; she surely is married by now. Why is it I think of Marianela when I see Yolanda?*

When he tried to sleep, the faces of the two unfortunate girls at Carlitos' house came to him. He shuddered, as he thought of their strange behavior.

He contemplated what Carlitos would attempt next and admonished himself to be more careful than ever as he went about his work.

The next morning Antonio lay abed, not wanting to leave the comfortable palette. He looked about the room, thinking, *It will suffice for me and my work. It is certainly ample for seeing people, even a whole family, in consultation.* As he waited for sunrise to start his daily prayers, there was a knock at his door. *My days seem to start with the unexpected,* he thought and went to answer it. Ramona was there. She was wrapped in a woolen cloak reaching to her ankles. Her head was covered with a scarf.

"May I come in before someone sees me standing here?" she begged.

"Come in!" Antonio motioned her toward the banco in his room and quickly shut the door. "What brings you here, Ramona?"

The girl removed her scarf and began pacing nervously. "I've run away from Carlitos. After you left yesterday, he made Christina and me follow you. She's deathly afraid to come to you for help and she returned with information of you. But I hid in the stable until now. I'm certain Carlitos is looking for me. I am afraid. Tell me what I must do!"

"Are you Arturo Montoya's daughter?" Antonio asked.

"I am, but I cannot ask my people for help. Carlitos would surely bring about my father's death. Carlitos told my father if I didn't help him, my father would be dead within a week. Please hide me so I don't have to return."

"You must not fear Carlitos any longer. Let me feed my horse and then I will walk with you and talk with your parents. You have made a wise decision. I hope Christina will do the same. Carlitos cannot usurp my power, nor can he overthrow my healing of your father."

"After you left yesterday, he raved like a crazy person. He beat Christina and me with his whip. My back is covered with welts," Ramona sobbed and she showed him Carlitos' handiwork.

When they knocked at the door of her parents' home, Yolanda let them in and the estranged sisters embraced.

"The power of love cannot be denied," Antonio said.

Yolanda told him, "You are making my father well. Now you have brought my sister home. You are a miracle-man, Antonio. Thank you," she said and bowed her head gratefully.

She added, "Before I forget, Señor Curandero, Señora Chavez asked for you to visit her today. She has a very sick child."

Yolanda gave Antonio directions to the Chavez' house. *My first patient is doing so well. Surely the villagers will hear of his progress and come to trust me,* he thought.

And so it was. The people kept Antonio very busy in the following weeks. With each patient, it was the same: Carlitos had given them the wrong herbs or decoctions and they grew worse. Then Carlitos would promise them they would get better and he would take their money and goods during their time of greatest desperation.

There was no time for Antonio to worry about Carlitos' next move against him. He had too much to do. But he felt an atmosphere of vengeance building and, although Carlitos himself was out of sight, his presence was felt by everyone.

Yolanda took an interest in Antonio's work and, with her husband's permission, she accompanied him on his visits to the people he was treating. This was invaluable to him for she knew each and every person. And, it pleased Antonio that she was interested in herbs. He began to teach her the power of the plants. There was a disquieting note, however, for when he had spent a lot of time with Yolanda, his thoughts turned to Marianela. When he had quiet moments alone, he thought: *What has happened to her? I feel sure she's married. And the good people of San Lucas? Will I ever have a clue as to my life before I met them?*

One still, starlit summer night, Antonio was returning from the home of a sick woman who lived near Carlitos' house. The piñon that dotted the small hills looked like soldiers standing sentinal. He imagined he saw some of them moving, marching toward him. There was a loud crashing noise and the soldiers collided, disrupting the quiet of the night.

Turning quickly, Antonio saw three figures rushing toward him. Before he could take a defensive stance, he was thrown to the ground.

Carlitos' dogs pinned him to his back. Their eyes in the darkness appeared red and they gnashed their teeth, drooling with excitement. Then Antonio felt a foot press on his neck—Carlitos—he felt the foot bear down.

Carlitos' voice was toneless: "I want you to get up and kneel before me and beg for your life. If you refuse, you are a dead man!"

Antonio gasped, "You are the one who must beg," and with a sudden twist of his body, he sprang to his feet and took the stance Juanito had taught him. "Your dogs are harmless." Antonio said. But even before he said it, as he was in midair and the dogs were leaping for his throat, something seemed to call them back, an invisible power. Now they were on all fours, licking their paws unconcernedly.

"Attack," Carlitos screamed in rage.

The two dogs went on with their licking.

Then Antonio reached within himself and called forth the power of José. His body crackled with a strange green glow. For a moment he stood motionless and Carlitos could see he was several inches off the ground, towering over him. Carlitos fell to his knees in supplication. His voice was that of a babbling child.

"Master," he sputtered, "Oh, master, please spare me."

"No one fears you anymore," Antonio's voice rumbled with power.

"That's not true. . ." Carlitos wept.

"The wealth you have acquired will be distributed among those from whom you have taken it. Do you understand, Carlitos?"

"I, I can't move," Carlitos stammered.

"Promise to leave Dolores this same night or you will remain crouched like a mouse for the rest of your life."

"I will do as you say," Carlitos whispered in defeat.

Then he slithered into the night, his dogs at his heels playful as pups.

Antonio watched him go. Would Juanito approve of such force? *I promised to rid Dolores of Carlitos, but I shouldn't have done it like this.* He took a deep breath.

Immediately Juanito's voice said to him, "You have now become José. Do not fear your strength or you will lose it."

At dawn the following day, Antonio heard a loud knock on his door. It was Christina; she was out of breath. "Señor, come quickly!" she called.

Before she could tell him more, Yolanda and a group of men appeared behind her. All were in a state of alarm.

"Come quickly, Antonio!" Yolanda shouted.

Throwing on his clothes, he grabbed his medicine bag and followed.

The crowd flowed quickly over the hills. Soon they came upon a small promontory which gave an excellent view of the valley Carlitos had inhabited. Flame and black smoke poured out of the house.

"Do you think Carlitos is in it?" Yolanda asked.

"No. If he were inside, he is gone now," Antonio answered.

The villagers watched the flames envelop the house. A column of smoke filled the sky. In a short while only the remains of adobe walls stood in the scarred place where the house had been hidden.

"It looks like the devil walked this way," one of the villagers said.

"An end to the devil!" said another.

Antonio stood by, silent, thoughtful.

"Not a single raven flies over this scene of devastation." Yolanda said. She added, "You were thinking of Christina just then, weren't you?" Her eyes filled with tears. "I don't believe we'll ever see Christina again."

Antonio watched the smoke. "Have faith." he said.

Later in the day, when the villagers and Antonio searched through the charred ruins, they found all the ingots of gold and silver.

"Divide it amongst those who lost it," Antonio advised.

Turning to Yolanda, he said, "I pray the villagers will never again permit anyone to victimize them. What they have seen today should serve to remind them."

"After seeing such a fire consume Carlitos' evil, I'm sure they won't forget," she replied.

They walked toward the house where a young mother was about to give birth to her first baby. "I wonder if it will be a boy or a girl," Yolanda asked.

"On such a day, it will be whatever she wishes. The power of goodness over evil is infinite," Antonio said. But he thought of Christina. "Carlitos must have told Christina to go home. He wouldn't dare harm her."

That evening the cousins were reunited. Christina appeared at her aunt and uncle's home wearing a smudged and ashen nightdress, her tear-streaked face a bitter reminder of the havoc Carlitos had wreaked upon this simple family. They rejoiced, all of them, and they toasted her return and the return to health of her uncle who was no longer bedridden.

Antonio remained eight years in Dolores. Word of his unusual healing powers and his gentleness with people made him a famous and much-sought-after curandero. Many people came to his door just to talk to him.

One day Yolanda asked, "Am I ready to be called a curandera?"

"I want to observe more of your healing before I deem you a curandera.

For the present, since you are involved only with physical healing, you are still a hermana saludera," he answered.

"I underestand, Antonio. I'm proud to be a healing sister—your pupil."

"When I left Juanito, I was barely a curandero. But because I had to search within for my hidden self in order to rid Dolores of Carlitos, I became something more than I was; I became a true curandero. Juanito had told me it would come about this way."

"You are so often pensive, Antonio. I wonder where your thoughts are, but I never dare ask."

"I don't intend to be removed," he answered with a kindly smile. "Well, speaking of Juanito brought back memories of him. . .and the others I knew before I came to Dolores. . .those who once depended on me."

With a deep sigh, he continued, "It bothers me I have no memory of my life before I found myself in the house of Don Miguel."

"So there is still a missing self hiding from you," Yolanda smiled.

In the months that followed, a smallpox epidemic raged through all of northern New Mexico. In San Lucas, people of all ages were stricken. Those who weren't afflicted helped to tend the sick and bury the dead. Don Miguel and Don Crescencio arranged for curanderos to visit the sick. They bought food—especially fresh fruit—for those who were bedridden. Their wives provided bedding and everyone in the village prayed the scourge would stop.

Marianela worked with young children, the ones who fell prey to the dread disease most easily. One afternoon as she sat with another woman who was helping nurse the sick, she lamented, "When will all this suffering, this severing of families, end. I feel so helpless."

"I look at that little sick girl in the house and ask, Dear God! Why is this necessary? These poor little ones just beginning life, just starting to serve You! Why take them?" her companion enjoined.

"It doesn't seem to make sense, does it? But then, we must trust in God," Marianela said.

"You look tired. Why don't you rest a while. . .I'll tend to our patient."

"Thanks, but I couldn't. To tell the truth, I haven't been able to sleep lately. Each time I drowse off, I remember someone who needs me."

You must get some sleep. You mustn't drain your energy, Marianela. You are badly needed. Everyone relies on us."

Since the village was within walking distance of their hacienda, Dona Rosamaria had invited Marianela to stay with the Ortiz family. When Dona Thomasita came to the village, she cautioned Marianela to get more rest. "You look so pale, dear. Aren't you eating?"

"I have no appetite, mother."

One afternoon, both Dona Rosamaria and Dona Thomasita demanded she lie down. "Try to rest, sleep, Marianela. You must!" Dona Rosamaria had given her Antonio's old room in the hacienda.

As she lay on his bed she looked at all his old belongings which his mother had thoughtfully left in place. She recalled the days that she and Antonio had spent before the accident. *The love we shared—how can it be forgotten? I will never love another. But I feel so. . .tired and dizzy*, and thinking this to herself, she lay awake as the room spun in circles and the bed, Antonio's bed, revolved and pitched and tilted so that she felt she was on a wicked sea.

By the time Dona Rosamaria knocked on her door next morning, Marianela's fever had risen and she was shaking uncontrollably. Dona Rosamaria sent for Martina and her daughter Gloria, who was now also a curandera.

"Don't worry. I'm just weak," Marianela whispered, her pale face shone with perspiration.

Marianela grew worse and worse and as the days wore on she slipped into a coma. Martina tried her herbal powers to no avail. La Concha was sent for and tried her own dark powers to drive the fever away, but there was no change in the stricken young woman. Don Crescencio decided to send for Juanito. When his messenger returned empty-handed, he was told: "Juanito cannot be found. Some say he has left on a long journey. No one seems to know where."

Dona Thomasita wept. "What shall we do? There must be a healer who will help my poor girl."

Antonio is still at Dolores," the messenger told them.

"My son," Don Miguel exclaimed. "Go and tell him at once."

"He has become quite a famous healer," the messenger said. "They say he never leaves Dolores."

"He will return, I know. He is one of us," Don Miguel replied.

The fastest horseman in San Lucas was dispatched with the message and the man arrived at Dolores by the next sun-up.

As he listened to the vaquero tell of Marianela's sudden illness, memories of the lovely girl with the dancing eyes came back to Antonio.

"Tell them I will be there soon after you arrive. Tell them to bathe Marianela with a warm, strong tea of verdolagas."

He watched the vaquero ride off into the hills toward San Lucas and then he went to Yolanda's house. She was with her husband tending their garden.

"I must speak with you, Yolanda."

"You look shaken!"

"I've just had bad news. . .a very dear person in San Lucas has been stricken. . .I must go to the village."

"That will leave Dolores without a curandero!"

Antonio looked into Yolanda's startled eyes. "It is time, I believe, that you must assume the duties of a curandera," he told her.

"But do you believe I am ready, Antonio?" She hoped he would not detect the sadness she felt at his leaving.

"I do," he replied. "Besides, you must. You will remember all I have taught you. You have been a good student."

"How long will you be away?" She dreaded the answer.

"I do not know."

"I know you will heal whoever it is and return to us quickly."

"I do not know," he answered and for the first time in many years, Yolanda could not discern the meaning of his answer.

Before he left, she took his hand and said, "You have given me what no other person could give. I will miss you, Antonio."

When she watched him leave, she wondered, *Did he read in my eyes how I feel toward him?*

Antonio arrived in San Lucas while the church bell was tolling. "How many dead?" he asked a man as he rode into the Ortiz courtyard. But the man just shook his head and said nothing.

Miguel spied his son and immediately ran to him. "Antonio. Thank God you are here! How good you look to these old eyes! We've missed you!"

"It is good to see you, too, Don Miguel," Antonio answered, feeling the warmth of the man who called him son.

"Marianela is not any better—but she has not become worse since they've started bathing her with the verdolaga tea. Let me take you to her. She is in your old room."

Marianela lay very still. *No color. And so thin!* Antonio thought when he first saw her. Her lovely, long hair was rolled back to keep it out of her face which was turned toward the wall. *She's still beautiful!*

Antonio didn't recognize the old woman who sat next to the bed. "It's Antonio, Emma," Don Miguel told her, "he wishes to be alone when he examines Marianela."

Emma muttered her disapproval and left reluctantly.

The curandero stood by Marianela and prayed. "May the Creator help me return you to healthy life!"

Then he took her hand and felt her pulse; he felt her brow for the degree of fever. He noted her breathing was slow and that she was in a deep sleep, but not a coma. Listening to her heartbeat with his ear to her chest, she moved slightly, moaned and opened her eyes.

Antonio said, "It is your. . .friend, Marianela. Remember me, Antonio? I am here to help you get well."

She blinked her eyes again, smiling faintly, trying to speak.

"You are going to be well soon," he said and to his surprise, she nodded. Then her eyes closed and she was deep asleep.

Hurrying to the kitchen, Antonio almost stumbled over Emma. "I'm glad you keep watch over her, Emma. Please stay with her until I return."

Amidst the fond embraces and greetings of the two families who had congregated to meet him, Antonio went about making medicines from his bag. To their questions, he confirmed, "It is smallpox. But she has a good chance. We must move quickly and start the treatments."

Dona Thomasita remained to assist him, saying to the others, "Why don't all of you wait for us in the sala? We will be helped more if you are out of the way."

The two of them prepared curative teas, poltices and salves from the bundles of herbs and ground powders encased in muslin bags.

"This is silver sage, or istafiate; this is powdered alamo suaco. . ." Antonio explained to Thomasita as he worked. "While we are waiting for these to brew, I'll prepare a salve which contains powdered chamiso blanco mixed with lamb fat. Would you boil water and get some small washcloths, please?"

In Marianela's room, Antonio said: "Place these hot towels on her stomach and chest." That done, Dona Thomasita slowly dripped the tea into the girl's mouth while Antonio held her lips open.

"We mustn't let the towels get cold. Perhaps Emma could get more hot water? The hot towels will relax her abdomen and chest making it easier for her to swallow." After they had gotten a cup of the tea down her throat, Antonio told Dona Thomasita: "I will leave you while you perform the last part of the treatment. You must cover all the sores on her body with the salve. Try not to miss any part."

Later Dona Thomasita looked in disbelief when she saw her daughter's eyes open wide. "She hasn't done that in over a week!"

"Don't try to speak, Marianela. It is I, Antonio. You are going to be all right. Rest. We won't leave you," Antonio said reassuringly.

Marianela closed her eyes again, but she reached out for Antonio's hand and held it. Smiling, Antonio turned to Dona Thomasita. "Tell the others. I will remain with her for a while. I want someone to stay with her until the second treatment."

When Dona Thomasita left, Antonio fell to his knees and gave thanks.

"Creator of all things, thank You for being allowed to reach Marianela in time and for the signs her body has shown to the initial efforts to heal her." He took her hand and he felt the healing warmth radiating within her.

Of the times he had dealt with smallpox before, he had been able to help people through the illness, but there had also been many failures. The warmth emanating from Marianela told him this was not going to be one of the failures. As he watched her, he wondered, *Is it possible she still cares for me after all these years?*

On the third day, encouraging changes took place. She was awake most of the day. The fever appeared to be lessening, the lesions were starting to heal, and she was able to drink the liver broth Antonio brought her. Through the nights, Antonio continued his vigil at her bedside.

"Your hand is so soothing, Antonio, when you massage my neck and arms," she whispered.

"You must conserve your strength. There will be plenty of time to talk."

"Thank God, I'm still alive and you are here! Tell me about you. . .all the things that have happened since you left." So he recounted the incidents of his life in Dolores and although she seemed to sleep or drowse while he spoke, he knew some part of her was listening to everything he said.

On the fourth morning, he came to her room, there was a sparkle in her eye, she smiled brightly. "What a change! Marianela, you look as if you could jump out of that bed."

"The cobwebs are gone from my mind. I'm "awake!" Not dreaming! Sometimes I thought it was all a dream. A bad, bad dream," she confessed.

With Marianela's recovery evident, both families—in fact the entire village—rejoiced. Antonio was treated like royalty returned. One afternoon, while Marianela napped, he began to assess what he felt was happening to him. *I feel an emotional mist that doesn't lift when I'm near her. It isn't her beauty . . .the lovely smile and dancing eyes or gentle voice. . . but the beauty within her. She's captured my heart. I've been so busy trying to keep her well, this is the first time I've thought how close I feel to her, how much I care for her.*

When she awoke and reached for his hand, she said, "I was having a wonderful dream. We were walking like we used to, years ago. Just you and I, hand in hand. We were talking about plants. You told me about herbs and their uses. Then suddenly a rainstorm! We ran quickly to this cave and climbed in. There was a mother coyote and her pups inside. They didn't seem to mind the intrusion and we shared the shelter until the storm abated. They seemed to accept our presence wholly, as if we belonged." After a moment of wonderment, she asked, "What do you think this dream means?"

"Perhaps the dream is telling you that we have finally learned to accept ourselves; that now we are ready to know each other, no matter how different our lives have been or in which direction our paths have taken us previously. I want you to know—and this comes from me, not the dream—I can now understand why I wanted to marry you. In this time I've been healing you, Marianela, I have fallen deeply in love with you."

Marianela reached out for him and Antonio sank into her arms. She drew his head to her breast. Not without tears, she sobbed, "Antonio! Antonio! I love you more than ever. You are my life and you always will be. The waiting is over, my prayers are answered! Now we will be together forever."

"I am so much in love with you. I thank God I have experienced the true feeling of love and not a counterfeit." As he looked into her eyes, there was a fleeting moment of sadness that came over him.

"I still don't remember what happened before," he said. "But that doesn't matter. We will make this the first and last—the present is all that matters."

It came, therefore, as no surprise to either family when Antonio and Marianela announced their intention to marry.

"What strange turns life takes!" Miguel remarked to his wife as they discussed the marriage plans.

"My fondest hope now is for Antonio to regain his memory," Rosamaria sighed.

"Perhaps it will come about, once he is married and remains home with us. Familiarity may help. . ." Miguel said.

One day Antonio told Marianela of the details of his life after he left San Lucas. "It was an important time in my life. It enabled me to become a curandero. I am deeply indebted to Juanito who is such a great teacher. I must thank him for the strength he gave me at Dolores. Through him, I found myself, through which I found you. I must go to find Juanito someday. Will you go with me, Marianela?"

"I want to meet him and the others."

"Perhaps it would make a special luna de miel?"

"I would love that, as much as I love you!"

The epidemic was over and church bells rang out for Antonio's and Marianela's wedding. The townspeople put aside their mourning for this happy occasion.

The church was crowded—some stood outside—as Marianela walked down the aisle. Silently she prayed and gave thanks for her answered prayers and she gazed on Antonio who stood waiting for her at the altar.

She approached and he took her hand, their eyes met, each smiling triumphantly. When the old padre recited the ceremony, he thought, *There is something special about these two. It is so they really love each other.*

When the priest pronounced them man and wife, the newlyweds knelt to pray and give thanks as the mass continued.

Before they rose, Antonio took a scroll, tied with red ribbon, from his vest and gave it to his bride. "I love you," he whispered as she took the paper.

"I have written you a wedding poem."

Unrolling it, she began to read those familiar words from the past:

We will walk hand in hand
over the meadows of Life,
Seeking to make our love grow
with each passing day.

Together we shall share all God's creations,
And loving care give to them,
As He has given us one-to-another.

When our work is done here on earth,
Lovers everywhere will sing our song.
An endless melody and tune,
With words that speak of love
which has no end.